ESSEX

IN THE FIRST WORLD WAR

Michael Foley

ESSEX

IN THE FIRST WORLD WAR

MICHAEL FOLEY

The
History
Press

To First Step, a pre-school setting for babies and children with special needs
and their families.
For being there for so many people
when no one else was.

I would like to express my thanks to Simon Donoghue of the Havering Library
Service for his help in making available the means of research for this book.
I happened to write this book during a spate of local library modernisations
which made research quite difficult and without Simon's help it would have
taken much longer to finish.

Also by Michael Foley

Front-Line Essex

More Front-Line Essex

Essex: Ready for Anything

Front-Line Kent

Front-Line Suffolk

Front-Line Thames

Hard as Nails

First published 2009

The History Press
The Mill, Brimscombe Port
Stroud, Gloucestershire, GL5 2QG
www.thehistorypress.co.uk

British Library Cataloguing in Publication Data.
A catalogue record for this book is available from the British Library.

ISBN 978-07524-5178-7

Typesetting and origination by The History Press
Printed in Great Britain

CONTENTS

INTRODUCTION

The history of Essex during the First World War is very different story to the account that I wrote of the county in the Second World War. There are several reasons for this, the main one being that there was not the same level of civilian danger in the First World War as there was in the later conflict, although in many cases the danger from air raids did seem to be the cause of a great deal of panic, and to present more risk than it actually did.

For the most part, in the more rural areas of the county the people who stayed at home were hardly touched by the conflict at all. There was also little news of the war in the more remote areas and apart from those who left to fight, the First World War must have seemed much like earlier wars when the fighting took place overseas and had little impact on the local population.

The more urban areas, of course, did suffer from the results of the war. The bombing of civilians was a new and terrifying experience for those who experienced it. Thankfully, the number of casualties was relatively low, at least in the early years of the war. There were also major changes in the population in the built-up areas of the county. Army camps sprang up all over Essex and while in many areas young men all but vanished as they rushed to join the armed forces, in others they were very evident and made up a majority in the local populace. Many of the new soldiers were also billeted in the homes of the local population, again bringing the war closer to home.

Not only was there an influx of men from the other parts of the country (strange enough in itself when working class people rarely travelled beyond their own towns), there were also men from the colonies who came to help the old country against the enemy. In some cases the men who came to fight must have looked very unusual indeed to the local population.

The experience of Essex's population of the war was varied. The inhabitants of a town like Colchester experienced the vast expansion of the population with thousands of young men converging on their town, bringing the problems that this created with them. Then there were the rural residents of small villages whose life went on as it had for many years before and whose news relating to the war was often sporadic and out of date.

INTRODUCTION

When I first began to research this book I believed that the Essex of the First World War period was far removed from the county we know today. This is in many cases true, especially relating to technology, but as I read about the rise in teenage pregnancy, the youth of the day being softer than their forefathers, the state doing too much for people and a shortage of nurses owing to poor pay, I began to think that perhaps life has not changed as much as we think it has. This then is what makes the story of Essex in the First World War such a varied and interesting one. ·

Michael Foley, 2009
www.authorsites.co.uk/michaelfoley

ONE

1914

The world in 1914 was a very different place to that which we know today. What we take for granted in the twenty-first century was in many cases unthought of at the time. In medicine there were no antibiotics to treat infections, so even the smallest wound could be fatal for an unlucky victim. Indeed it was only in 1914 that the first non-direct blood transfusion was carried out by the Belgian surgeon Albert Hustin.

The rights of members of the general population were not as clear-cut in the pre-war period as they are now; certainly not in this country or in other supposedly civilised states. In April 1914 the Colorado Coalfield massacre took place when the United States National Guard attacked a colony of 1,200 striking miners living in tents and killed twenty-four of them.

There was very little news of the outside world in the more remote areas; radio was in its infancy and newspapers were only available in urban areas. Even travel was difficult, as in many cases the railway had not yet reached rural areas and travel was still mainly dependent on the horse. This then was the background against which the war began.

The causes of the First World War are complicated and involve a number of factors. There have been several long books written about this and many of them still disagree over the exact cause. It is obvious that there were severe problems among the smaller states of Europe and as the larger powers pledged their support to these states, they usually had their own interests in mind, so they came into conflict.

Then there were the ambitions of the larger powers in adding to their colonies. The assassination of the Archduke Ferdinand is often seen as the cause of the war, but this was just the spark that set off the powder keg that was Europe in 1914.

The actual conflict began with Austria attacking Serbia. The larger powers then aligned themselves; Russia, France and Britain (the Triple Entente) against Austria-Hungary, Italy and Germany (the Triple Alliance). On 1 August Germany declared war on Russia, on the 3rd against France and on the 4th against neutral Belgium. England declared war on Germany in support of Belgium, then German troops invaded Belgium and swept through the country into France. The British forces that could be mustered at this time numbered less than 200,000 and were sent to France in early August. The Germans called them a 'contemptible little army' and the name stuck as the 'old contemptibles'.

The British were first stationed at Mons in Belgium near the French border. They were quickly forced to retreat by the advancing German Army and it was not until mid-September that they finally halted the German advance at the River Marne. That was when the first trenches were dug and were to set the pattern of the war.

The first Allied victories came in October and November at Ypres. The Germany Army was held and then began the stalemate that was to last for most of the war with small gains for each side, usually at the cost of thousands of lives. Turkey entered the war in October on the German side.

Christmas 1914 saw the well-known unofficial truce between the Germans and the British when the men met in no man's land and, for a short time at least, the war was forgotten (at least by the lower ranks if not by the senior officers). There were games of football and gifts exchanged, along with views of the war from both sides. For the first time many of the British soldiers found out that although they thought their cause was the right one, so did the enemy.

❖ ❖ ❖

The Beach, Southend-on-Sea. 6096.

When war broke out, public transport to places like Southend was much more difficult to use as it was taken over for military use.

Although the railway had made inroads into many parts of Essex, by the outbreak of war travel between the railway stations was not easy. New stations were being added to the county up until the war began but this then stopped once the fighting started. The availability of public transport by train actually decreased on some lines as military traffic took priority. The government took control of the Fenchurch Street line to Southend and any available tickets for the public were much more expensive than they had been before the war. Women were also employed on the railway for the first time, as they were in many other industries.

Another seemingly simple aspect of rail travel that changed during the war was the vending machines that stood on station platforms; there were always chocolate machines and others that printed your name on small metal strips for a penny. These unusual luxuries made rail trips so interesting for the young passengers. As the war progressed these machines were always empty, taking away some of the magic of rail travel for children.

Cars were still rare in Essex, as were buses. In the larger towns electric trams had been running for some time, which was a cheap form of travel for the working classes. It was still the case, however, that workers normally lived close to their place of work, even in the more built-up areas. If they used any type of transport to get to work it was usually a bicycle.

The county of Essex was a varied place in 1914. In the west of the county, near to London, the spread of the capital had led to an increase in industry. Much of what we now think of as the East End of London was then several small towns

Some towns in Essex had a tram system, such as this one in Colchester.

It must have been an exciting and unusual experience for trippers to take a ride along the sea front on a tram at Thorpe Bay.

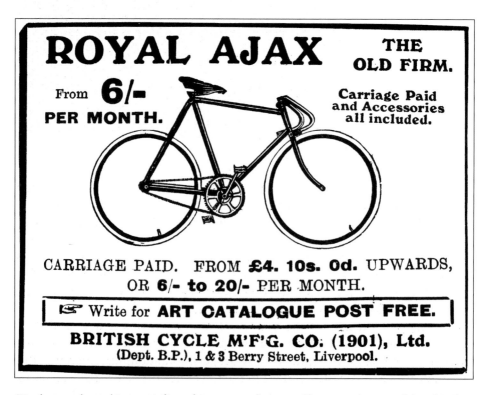

Bicycles were the working man's form of transport as the reasonable terms to buy one of these bicycles shows.

Bicycles may have been a cheap form of transport for the working classes, but they were a form of recreation for the better off too.

in Essex, but the spread of the capital had begun to join them into one large mass. Barking had lost its old reliance on the fishing industry and farming and had turned to newer, more modern and, often, just as lethal industries mainly based around the site of what had been the centre of its fishing industry, Barking Creek. This transition was true of other towns, too. It was along rivers such as the Roding, Bow Creek and the Thames that much of the early industry settled. Water transport was still a major factor in this as many goods were still carried by barges or larger boats.

Many of the industries of the time were not run with the health of their employees in mind. Match manufacture had been present in the town of Barking for a number of years and despite its early dangers, conditions had improved. But a new industry, Cape Asbestos, arrived in the town the year before the war began. It was only to be many years later that the danger of working with asbestos was to lead to the town having the highest death rates from asbestosis in the country.

Some industries were dangerous for the health of their workers. The match industry had improved by this time and many of the labels on the boxes, such as this one made at Barking, had a patriotic theme.

The area around Bow Creek, like Barking, was also the site of numerous factories producing items such as chemicals. The processes often led to widespread pollution of the river and the local atmosphere. Lax regulations by local councils were one of the reasons that the sites for these lethal factories were chosen. The unpleasant smells from these industries must have made life unbearable at times for the local communities.

Despite the dangers of industry, there had been attempts to improve the health of the population, especially after the poor condition of the men who were needed for service in the Army during the Boer War. Barking was well advanced in this and the majority of homes in the town had a water supply; not something that was common in the rest of the county. Despite this, health was still an issue in Barking. In the years before the war infant mortality was twice the rate in Barking than that in Ilford. This was mainly the result of poverty. Although the National Insurance Act had been passed in 1911 which made payments to the sick and unemployed who had paid contributions, this did not cover all workers. Even those who were covered only had benefits for a limited period. The difference in infant mortality rates between towns that were so close also shows how varied life in the county could be.

Colchester was one of the towns which had a wide-reaching system of electric trams since 1904. There were a number of industries in the town such as engineering and iron foundries. As well as supplying a home for the troops the town also helped to provide the goods for war that the men needed. While the engineering factories turned to armament production during the war, clothing factories were producing uniforms for the troops.

Much of the early industry in Barking was based around the town quay and relied on water transport.

Although trams ran in Colchester, horses and carts or even handcarts were still the more common form of transportation.

Ilford was a much healthier place to live than nearby Barking becuase the population there were better off. Some had enough money to build grand houses such as this, which was not as old as it looked.

The radio masts at Marconi's factory were more than 400ft high. They must have been a useful guide for German airships.

Chelmsford had a rather unusual range of factories. Marconi had opened the first radio factory in the town in 1898, which was then rebuilt in 1912. In 1913 two 453ft masts were erected.

In 1902 Clarkson & Capel Steam Bus Syndicate had begun to build steam buses in the town. Although the Great Eastern Railway Company ran petrol buses to their stations in the area from 1905, in 1913 they were replaced by steam buses. There were also a number of steam-driven lorries in use in the town.

Moore brothers of Kelvedon ordered a double-decker steam bus from Clarkson's and it was delivered in 1914. The bus ran from Kelvedon to Colchester and was the first self-propelled bus to run in the area. It travelled at 12mph and the solid tyres must have made the journey very uncomfortable for its passengers. By the end of the war however, petrol-driven vehicles were once more growing in popularity.

Steam vehicles could also be quite dangerous. It was believed that sparks from a steam lorry could have been responsible for a fire that broke out at Bordeaux Farm, Little Chesterford, in April 1914. The fire spread to Manor Farm and then to the village, destroying farm buildings, cottages and two public houses.

Inhabitants in more rural parts of Essex had a very different lifestyle to those living in the towns. Although there was poverty in the urban areas, in some parts of the countryside poverty was very bad indeed. For many rural people the staple diet was bread and potatoes with what ever they could grow for themselves in gardens or allotments. Work on their own plot often followed long hours in the fields of their employer.

The levels of poverty suffered by the population during the war are a matter for debate. The commonly held view is that because of the need for longer hours in industry and the shortage of food that meant more work for farmers, everyone was better off. This was no doubt true of those who went into the Army and their families. In some cases the war came as a financial relief for those men who did not have regular work – when they joined the Army they received regular, if low, pay. Their families also received separation allowances, which again were low, but were better than nothing.

There was so much hardship among some families that regular trips to the pawnshop were a necessity. When soldiers arrived home on leave they often found that they had no civilian clothes to wear as they had all been pawned. Even bedding was pawned in the worst cases.

When men joined the Army from the rural areas it was often an improvement financially as they would receive regular wages, which was not always the case for some farm workers. This also left those who had not joined up in a better position as there were fewer men and therefore more work available.

For women who could not go out to work, doing the laundry for local soldiers was an alternative. Huge amounts of dirty uniforms could be delivered to a house and then collected when clean. Soldiers at the large camps often helped out the locals by passing food over the fences to children.

Many of the small hamlets in the county had no shops or pubs of their own. Schools for the children were often miles away and the only way to get there

Much of the work on farms was still carried out by horses rather than machines.

was to walk and many of the children had no shoes. Spike Mays wrote how one boy at his school wore his father's old Essex Regiment uniform altered to fit, as he had no other clothes. The walk to school was not only made during the week, as most children would also go to Sunday school. There was often a choice of churches in the local area and on a Sunday morning the sound of church bells could be heard from many different sources depending on the wind direction.

Families were often large, as the idea of widespread contraception was still in its infancy. The only reason that the numbers of children were kept down was the high infant mortality. Births would be attended by unqualified but experienced midwives who would also help out after the birth for a price.

There would normally be a village near smaller hamlets, which would have some amenities. Ashdon, a village close to Saffron Walden, had five pubs but only two shops; both were grocer's shops but one was also a post office. Although called grocer shops, they actually sold everything that the locals would need such as clothes, paraffin and tobacco.

Some men were excused from serving in the forces if their work was important to the farms; for example, tractor drivers who were rare as most farm-work was still carried out using horses. These men were given armbands to show that they were in reserved occupations, otherwise they ran the risk of people accusing the them of being cowards.

In Dunmow, as in many areas, the outbreak of war was announced by a notice in the post office window. Although news of the war may not have been available

Many children lived in large, poor families but the children at Great Saling School just after the war look to be well clothed and fed.

in the area on a regular basis, the sound of the guns in France was a constant reminder of the conflict. Plans were drawn up to evacuate the local population from the area in the result of an invasion. The citizens of Dunmow would go to Oxford and there would be farm carts allocated for the use of the elderly, the sick and children. Everyone else would have to walk. Whether there would actually be enough carts for this use was debatable, especially as so many horses had been commandeered for Army use.

There did not seem to be a great deal of fear about invasion, not like there had been in previous wars or like there would be in 1939. Despite the lack of fear over invasion however, the thought of being bombed by Zeppelins was much more frightening for the population than the actual danger from them.

Despite the fear that they caused, there also seemed to be a fascination with the airships. A description of a sighting of a Zeppelin was given by Charles Perfect in his book *Hornchurch in the Great War.*

> There was a silvery object, the shape of a huge cigar caught in the rays of dozens of searchlights. Whichever way it turned the searchlights followed it making it a clear target for the guns.

Hornchuch itself was described by many as a town but has also been called a village. One of the largest industries in the town at the time of the war was

Small pictures, such as this one of Burnham-on-Crouch, were often used as rewards for children's attendance at Sunday schools.

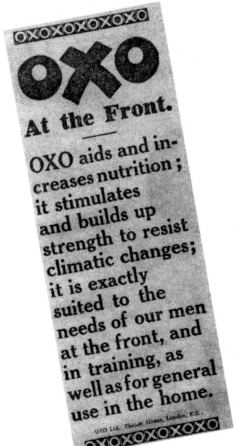

Companies were not averse to using the war as a means to sell their goods as this advertisement for Oxo shows.

the Hornchurch Brewery. They had thirty horses, which pulled the drays that delivered to the large number of public houses that the brewery owned in Essex. The horses were kept in a field behind the King's Head public house.

Housing in the countryside was normally much more primitive than in the towns. Very few houses had running water and lighting was usually provided by oil lamps. People living in these houses knew no different as most of them spent their whole lives working on local farms and rarely travelled further than the local village or nearest town. Even those living in nearby hamlets or villages were often viewed with suspicion.

One source of employment for the locals would often be the large estate of the local landowner, often on farms owned by the lord or as live-in domestic servants. There would also be opportunities for beaters when they held shooting parties for their rich friends. The local gentry were often the owners of the only car in the area.

Some claims made by companies in their advertisements may have been a little far-fetched.

Horsemen on farms were seen as a higher form of employee. They were hard to replace and often used this reason to get out of joining the forces.

Because of the close connection with the land, harvest time was the most important time of the year. There would be a large party, often paid for by the local squire. Much of the farm work revolved around horses, as tractors were still very rare.

The area around Basildon that included Laindon, Pitsea and Vange had been the source of an innovative scheme for some years. Small plots of land had been sold off for a number of years for a few pounds to people, mainly from London, who wanted a place out in the countryside. The type of homes that sprang up on these plots varied immensely from tents to wooden buildings no better than sheds and even old railway carriages. They were mainly used for holidays. Some, however, did build homes and lived in them permanently. During the war many people bought these plots with monthly payments of 10s or a pound. There was a similar scheme in operation on Canvey Island for a time.

There were other centres of population in the county that did not fit either the urban or rural pattern of common Essex towns and villages. One of these was Kynochtown at Shell Haven near Canvey Island. Kynoch and Company had opened an explosives factory on the site in 1895. The works had been greatly

Harvest time was an important event in rural Essex when everyone in the area became involved in some way.

expanded during the war and because of its remote position a town of wooden huts sprang up to house its predominantly female workforce. The huts were later replaced by brick-built houses. It became known as Kynochtown and had its own shop, a school and an institute.

There was another new development when the women at the factory formed a football team and played women's teams from other factories in Essex. Women were beginning to find that they could do things during the war that had not been possible beforehand. The Kynochtown site was often bombed and although trenches were dug for the workers' protection, they often went into the fields during raids instead of using the shelters.

The site was guarded by soldiers who kept away any suspicious strangers. There was an idea put forward by John Chessire, a member of the Sportsman's Battalion based at Hornchurch, to deal with attacks on the factory. He thought that German prisoners of war should be held at places like Kynochtown to deter the Germans from bombing their own men.

The memories of some of the workforce at Kynoch and Company were recorded. Catherine and Dorothy Mackintosh were sisters who worked at the factory and lived at Kynochtown during the war. They had to have a medical before they could start work there, as the occupation of munitions worker was a dangerous one. Whether this medical was any more thorough than the Army

A busy street scene in Leigh-on-Sea with signs of the times: a tram and a horse and cart.

medical is debatable. The sisters worked Monday to Saturday and did alternate day and night shifts for a week. The pay was four pence halfpenny an hour with time and a half for Saturday nights.

At first they lived in Stanford le Hope and were taken to work by lorry. They then moved to Corringham where a light railway ran to the works. Once they arrived at the site they changed into special safety clothes and shoes while still well away from the factory floor. Despite the safety clothes the fumes from cordite were sometimes so bad that workers passed out.

The sisters eventually moved to Kynochtown itself but called it the Colony. As well as providing the workers with a place to live there were also social events to take part in such as a historical pageant. An interesting comment from the girls concerned one weekend when they went home. When they came back they brought some stew, which contained some small potatoes from their father's allotment. The potatoes aroused a lot of interest among the other workers, as they were so rare at that time.

The experience of the Mackintosh sisters shows the reason that many did not travel far to work – the problem of transport. Where there were trains they were too expensive for the normal working man or woman to use every day. Where the trains did run, the workers in the fields could often know the time of day by the trains because they were so infrequent. Most travel and carriage of goods was still done by horse-drawn vehicles, as motorcars were also still rare at this time.

When war broke out, the large increase in the number of men joining the Army led to severe problems in finding them accommodation. Although Army

As well as building a factory and town for their workers, Kynoch and Company also built their own hotel.

A light railway was built to Kynochtown. This photograph shows the halt after it was taken over and became Coryton.

Although Hornchurch looks to have been a quiet village, it was full of a number of different troops during the war.

Although there were camps all over Essex, some of the Essex Regiment ended up in Halton Park Camp, Buckinghamshire, from where one of them sent this card.

She won't even look at anything under a Regimental Sergeant. Major.

There were attempts to make some things about the war more light-hearted.

camps were beginning to spring up all over the country, many soldiers were still billeted in peoples' homes.

In some cases this was very welcome, even for the well off. Ellen Wilmott of Warley Place was known internationally for her fine gardens. By the beginning of 1914 she was having severe financial difficulties and the war came as a blessing as some of her houses were used by soldiers, giving her a supplementary income. She also lost some of her gardeners to the forces which cut down on her expenses.

The less well off also welcomed the men billeted in their homes, as this was an additional source of income. There was also a lucrative sideline in letting rooms to the wives of soldiers who came to the area to visit their husbands in local camps.

The result of these men coming into towns and villages was that the newcomers often became very involved in the social life of the area. There would usually be halls where off-duty soldiers and civilians could mix and often entertainment would be provided by the locals and the troops themselves. When the men left the area to go and fight or move to a different camp, the locals often kept in touch or looked for news of the unit as they saw them as 'their' soldiers.

When the war broke out, the Essex Infantry Brigade, which was a territorial unit, were in their annual camp at Clacton. The men had been offered £1 if they stayed for fifteen days. Then war broke out and instead of going home they were sent off to make up the numbers in various regiments. There were around 3,000 men at the camp, which was an annual event and was situated between Little Clacton and Thorpe and was about 2½ miles from the sea front.

The group of men outside what looks to be a public house are obviously very interested in the photographer taking this shot of Mistley and its famous towers.

Sporting events at the big house were always popular events as this coursing meeting at Matching Hall shows.

The National Reserve had been a voluntary organisation for ex-members of the armed forces for a few years before the war began. Many of the members of the reserve went straight into the Army on the outbreak of war.

The war brought some unexpected activity to Clacton. Even the old Napoleonic Martello Towers in the town were occupied by the military. No doubt the men in the towers would have had a good view of an aircraft from the seaplane base at Felixstowe that was forced to land on the beach in the early days of the war. The plane's passenger was none other than Winston Churchill, who was quickly accosted by a crowd of suffragettes.

It was not only the regular Army that began to play its part in the defence of the country. There was a Volunteer Training Corps that was similar to the Home Guard of the Second World War. Men over the age of military service could join and younger men were also allowed to enlist so that they could get some military experience before they reached enlistment age for the regular Army.

In Colchester the Volunteer Force was commanded by Major White Hopkins. For the first few months of their existence they only had one rifle. They were later given carbines and short Japanese rifles.

The Volunteer Training Corps was later taken over by the War Office. It then became part of the territorials and everyone not in the military was asked to join. The volunteers would man local searchlight stations and Lewis gun sites releasing

The lack of modern conveniences in Essex homes is shown by the offer of a free booklet on the use of a gas cooker. They were rare enough for their use to be a mystery to most housewives.

Recruits were in camps all over the county as this Knuts of Purfleet Huts card shows. The soldier on the left of the front row looks very young.

regular soldiers for the trenches. The men were also sent on week-long training courses to Tadworth.

There were a large number of special constables enlisted to help the police. These men had to be ready to act in the event of an invasion by the enemy. They would be responsible for moving the local population out of an area and sorting out supplies for them. Their work also included checking that the blackout was enforced when air raids began.

Even youngsters were expected to join in with the war effort. Before the war began Viscount Haldane, the Minister of War, suggested that all youth organisations including the Boy Scouts were brought under control of the War Office. Although this never happened, the Scouts played their part as orderlies and messengers. They even guarded telegraph wires at night when there were fears over possible espionage by enemy aliens.

Badges were awarded for twenty-eight days' service of more than three hours a day. Two of the Scouts in Romford who helped out at Hare Hall Camp became very good friends with one of the men there. Raymond Williams and Albert Harper lived in Emerson Park and invited one of the soldiers they met back to their homes. His name was Wilfred Owen, a member of the Artist Rifles and one of the most famous of the War Poets.

The Church Lads' Brigade was also a much more military organisation than the Boys' Brigade of the more recent past. They also became part of the territorial force and in some cases became cadet battalions. The Voluntary Aid Detachments (VAD) were a mainly female-based voluntary organisation that took over much

The Church Lads, such as these at Hornchurch, were a much more military-based organisation during the war and were taken under the control of the War Office.

By the beginning of the war the Boy Souts were a popular organisation. They went on to play a big part in protecting the home front.

The barracks at Warley had been in use long before the First World War. The band entering the barracks seem to have drawn a large crowd.

of the work in the greatly increased number of hospitals. They ran canteens and recreation huts for the patients.

A great deal of the transport used to carry the wounded from train stations to hospitals was privately owned and manned by volunteers. The VAD were responsible for opening more than 600 new hospitals in the country during the war.

The VAD were not the only organisation involved in hospitals for the troops. On the outbreak of war the Duke of Sutherland's organisation for the registration and equipping of country houses as hospitals and convalescent homes for wounded soldiers was amalgamated with the Incorporated Soldiers' and Sailors' Help Society to avoid the two organisations' work being duplicated.

There were numerous fears over espionage early in the war and the newspapers were full of stories of suspicious characters. As early as 8 August 1914 there was a spy scare at Harwich. A man had arrived by boat from Holland and went round the harbour taking photographs. He was reported to have had the appearance of a German and it turned out that he had been born in Germany but was an American citizen. He was eventually allowed to carry on to New York.

Elsewhere in the county there were other reports of spies, although the following case had taken place a few months earlier but was reported after the war began. Mr Stephen Cooke of Ye Old Thatched House Hotel in Epping had reported strange men taking photographs of military establishments nearby and of showing interest in recently opened reservoirs in Chingford. It turned out that three of the men were German Army officers. Mr Cooke reported strange characters in the area after the war began as well.

Pier Approach and Bridge, Clacton-on-Sea

Everyone at the seaside seems to be dressed in their best clothes. For many, a day at Clacton may have been their only holiday for the year.

I'm enjoying my little self at **CLACTON-ON-SEA**

Building castles in the air
May be done just anywhere,
But for castles in the sand
This is indeed the happy land!

1085

This card from Clacton opened out to reveal eleven smaller images of the town.

As well as suspected spies, German prisoners were also arriving at Harwich as early as August. Germans were also proving to be a problem in other parts of the county when a German man and his chauffeur crashed their car into a horse and cart in Braintree. The newspaper headline made it clear that the man in the car was German.

It was not only in England where prisoners were being taken early in the war. One celebrity prisoner on the continent was the Bishop of Colchester. As with many holidaymakers of the time he was unaware of the situation between Britain and Germany and was happily enjoying his holiday. He was then arrested for taking a photograph. After being held for some time he was finally released and returned to Britain.

It was not only abroad that taking photographs was a cause for concern. A man from Seven Kings had been spending a holiday at Purfleet and returned home by train just after the war broke out. He decided to take a snapshot of the aeroplane tower that had been erected between Purfleet station and the rifle ranges. He was spotted by one of the guards and a message was relayed to Barking where he was arrested as the train arrived. After being held for a number of hours he was finally released, but his camera was confiscated.

There were, of course, already military barracks in the town of Colchester and these were to see a vast increase in the number of soldiers based there during the war. The regular soldiers moved out as the war began to be the first to go and fight. They were replaced by territorials and volunteers who arrived in the town, often with no uniforms and no weapons. The barracks were overflowing and

Cards like this one were printed for most of the camps in Essex. Some showed the image of a butler serving men lying in hammocks.

A badge of the Comrades of the Great War Organisation that was one of the forerunners of the British Legion.

A typical rural scene which makes it hard to imagine that this is a view of a country at war.

Hare Street, Gidea Park   No. 296

Hare Street was a small hamlet in Romford that was to become a hive of activity when troops were based at the new camp at Hare Hall.

soldiers were living in tents or billeted in peoples homes. At times the number of soldiers in the town almost equalled the civilian population, which was around 40,000. Other parts of the town began to be taken over; even Layer Road football ground was used as a parade ground.

In Chelmsford the landlord of the Woolpack Inn, Mildmay Road, a Mr William Young, was charged with unlawfully refusing accommodation to soldiers. His excuse in court was that the soldiers used filthy language in front of his son. The case was dropped.

Some areas that were later to become Army camps were put to a different use at this early point of the war. Hare Hall Park in Romford was later to be the home of the 2nd Sportsman's Battalion and the Artist Rifles. In August it was used for a hospital fête and gala to raise funds for the Victoria Cottage Hospital in the town. The hospitals were often run on gifts and fundraising activities. The fundraising event at Hare Hall Park included a horse show as well as the fête and gala. It was held on August bank holiday and the event showed how popular such amusements were for local people who had little else to occupy their time. There were over a 1,000 visitors described as holidaymakers at the show.

Cottage hospitals were quite common in the county. They usually had up to twenty-five beds and although the Workpeople's Contributions Scheme had begun in 1900 where people could pay a weekly contribution for treatment, money was still raised and donated by events such as the gala. The advantage of

Cottage hospitals were present in many Essex towns such as this one at Woodford. They mainly relied on voluntary contributions but were much busier during the war than they were in peacetime.

Purfleet Village, the rear of the hotel stands to the left and the barracks were beyond that.

cottage hospitals was that the patients were known by the local doctors who worked in them and many of them lasted up to the Second World War and beyond.

There are some personal memories of the war in existence; one of these was from Robert Taylor Bull whose diary is available in the Essex Record Office. He was living in Burnham when the war broke out and a few days later he travelled to Maldon to look at a cart. He mentioned that there were a large number of soldiers near Cold Norton. Carts seemed to be the common form of transport as he also recalls a visitor who arrived in a donkey cart.

The constant movement of men between camps was shown by the 10th Essex who were moved from Shorncliffe Camp in Kent to Colchester in October. They were described as arriving as a rabble, dressed in blue uniforms owing to the shortage of khaki, before marching out as a fine battalion in May 1915.

Even soap advertisements could use a patriotic theme to help sell it.

Soldiers' clubs such as this one in Chelmsford were set up all over the county to give the men somewhere to go, other than the pub.

The members of the battalion were from varied backgrounds. Men from the East End of London now rubbed shoulders with rural workers from the most remote parts of Essex and Suffolk.

Large numbers of recruits in the new camps was not uncommon; in Rainham, what was known as Rainham Musketry Camp was at one point occupied by around 10,000 recruits living in tents. The camp was actually on part of the firing ranges of Purfleet Barracks. The camp of volunteers far outnumbered the populations of the small local villages.

Every part of Essex seemed to have its own soldiers. West Ham Park became the drill ground for the Essex Artillery Territorials. They spent the days in the park and were billeted at Water Lane School in the evenings.

Billericay was the home of the 6th Warwickshire Regiment, most of whom had volunteered early in the war. After a short spell in the town they were led off by their band to the station, singing the patriotic songs of the day, from where trains took them on the first part of their journey to the battlefields of France. Billericay was also to be the home of other regiments later in the war including the Cameroonians, Scottish Rifles and the Border Regiment who were enlisted in Southend.

Burnham-on-Crouch was the home of the Gloucester Regiment, the Oxford & Bucks Light Infantry and the Army Cyclist Corps. The infantry took turns in guarding the coastline.

No doubt cards like this one of Chelmsford would have been sent to the families of numerous soldiers billeted in the town.

Purfleet was only a relatively small village but, apart from the barracks, it had a training ship and a hotel standing on the bank of the Thames that had been a popular place for visits from Londoners in boats.

There were some forms of entertainment for the newly arrived troops if they were lucky enough to be near to one of them. A cinema had opened in West Avenue, Clacton, in 1913. There was also a cinema at Kynochtown. The Empire cinema opened in Chelmsford during the war. Brentwood had the Electric Palace that opened in 1914, while the Picture Palace in Shoebury had opened in 1913. Another form of entertainment disappeared when the garrison theatre was taken over as a hospital at Shoebury. In Southend, films had been shown before the war in theatres but specialised cinemas came later.

The first signs of antagonism against anyone with German or Austrian origins were shown early in the war. The *Essex Times* reported as early as the end of August that German tradesmen in Stratford were being abused as traitors. Many tried to show their allegiance by displaying Union Jacks. The newspaper was at the time surprisingly sympathetic to the plight of the Germans. They were described as respectable citizens. This was a very different attitude to how the press were to later describe them.

The treatment of aliens by the authorities had begun to change by September and even the reports in the *Essex Times* had a slightly more sinister slant. When Humbert Housell, a German hairdresser from Marylebone, was arrested in Leyton he was charged with travelling more than 5 miles from his address. He said that he didn't know that he had travelled more than that distance. The report went on to mention that since his last registration he had shaved off the beard that he had previously worn.

Another German national from Canning Town was also arrested at the same time. Robert Kruger was sixty-eight years old and had lived in Britain for fifty years. He was charged with failing to register as an enemy alien. He thought that he was too old, but as it turned out there was no age limit.

Although it was later reported that crime had dropped since the war began there were still numerous felonies reported which were committed by both soldiers and civilians. In Barking, Elias Shoesmith of Factory Road was charged with grievous bodily harm on PC Preveet. He attacked the policeman while drunk and was sentenced to six months' hard labour.

A member of the 3rd Battalion Essex Regiment was charged with theft at Mistley. The soldiers were camping on a farm in the district and a goose and a cockerel went missing and were found half eaten at the soldiers' camp. Private Harry Cole was charged with the theft. He had been a member of the regiment for fifteen years and had an unblemished record. He was let off with costs.

There were attempts to provide an interesting and respectable pastime for the large number of soldiers that arrived in Essex. The British Woman's Temperance Association opened a soldiers' institute in Warley Road under the charge of the Revd Mr R. Whittleton. The institute was to provide writing materials, games and refreshments. No doubt the aim of the woman behind this was to keep the soldiers out of the local pubs. The report also asked for contributions of newspapers, magazines and stationery.

Another entertainment obviously enjoyed by members of the public as well as servicemen was a concert by the Scots Guards Band in Barking Park. There had

Holland-on-Sea was still undeveloped during the war, unlike its close neighbour Clacton.

Away from the sea front much of the area around Clacton was still rural and consisted of separate villages.

Prittlewell Village.

As with Clacton, away from Southend seafront the countryside was still very rural, as this scene of Prittlewell shows.

been previous concerts in the park but none had been as popular with a crowd reported to be around 10,000. Not only did they enjoy the occasion, they also joined in to sing such favourites as 'Abide With Me', 'Rule Britannia' and the national anthem.

The danger from enemy aircraft must have been in everyone's minds when two aeroplanes flew over Purfleet Camp and did not answer the challenge from the camp. The aeroplanes were then fired on and part of one of the shells weighing around 6lb fell to earth between the Rabbits beer house and Palmerston Cottages.

The shell narrowly missed Mrs Nose who lived at no.1 Palmerston Cottages, and sunk deep into the ground as it landed. The shell was kept by the landlord of the Rabbits, Mr Idle.

There was an unusual event in August at Forest Gate when two trams crashed. As trams ran on rails, crashes must have been very rare. A tram owned by the London County Council had fouled the points at Green Street and crashed into a tram owned by the West Ham Corporation, which was travelling in the opposite direction. Although both trams were badly damaged, injuries to the passengers and drivers were minor.

There was another unusual accident in North Stifford. Mr Vaughn, a local farmer, had been driving through the town in a horse and trap accompanied by his housekeeper Mrs Martindale. He stopped the trap by Mr Perry's shop and left Mrs Martindale in charge of it while he went inside. A young lady, Miss Jackson,

BRENTWOOD ELECTRIC PALACE,

HIGH STREET.

Resident Manager .... Mr. S. V. WILSON.

Continuous Performance 5.30 to 9.30. Matinee, Thursday and Saturday at 2.30. 'Phone 64.

SPECIAL !

THURSDAY, FEBRUARY 24th,

Albert Chevalier & Florence Turner

IN

MY OLD DUTCH.

Seats may be booked by 'phone between 10.30—1 and 5.30—9.30.

x24-33

Cinemas were beginning to appear in many Essex towns during the build up to war. It is interesting that the manager is named and that seats can be booked by telephone, which were rare during the war.

then came around the corner on a bicycle and crashed into the horse causing it to run off and making Mrs Martindale fall out of the trap. The pony was later stopped by a man in the town.

There was an interesting article in the *Essex Times* in September about a man named Samuel Odart of Whittaker Road, Upton Park. He had been born in 1813 and had therefore lived from the Battle of Waterloo until the First World War and was aged 101. He had been employed for more than fifty years as a silk weaver and had helped to make the scarf worn by Queen Victoria during her Coronation. Mr Odart was not to see much of the new war however as he died in late August.

There were some restrictions imposed in the county. All duck and wildfowl shooting was prohibited along the Thames from Tilbury Fort to Hole Haven. This was to have a serious effect on many families whose subsistence was reliant on this as a means of gaining food. The taking of photographs of any military site was forbidden which is strange when one considers the number of postcards of military sites that there are from this time.

Harwich became one of the few restricted areas in the county as the port became a naval base; the home of the Harwich Force under Admiral Tyrwhitt. Visitors were restricted from entering the town. Any person wanting to enter had to register their occupation and address.

A form was given to hotel and lodging housekeepers in Harwich that had to be filled in with the details of any guest staying with them. As well as address and

INSTRUCTIONS FOR OBTAINING A PERMIT BOOK.

NOTE.—A first Permit Book is issued free. For each further Book issued, or for the restoration by the Police of a lost book, a charge of One Shilling is made.

1. Fill in the application form opposite, and repeat these particulars on page 1.

2. Affix your photograph in the spaces provided on the application form and on page 1, and hand the book to the Police Officer to stamp the photographs.

3. The Police will remove and retain this application form and will return you the book to take away.

4. The purposes for which Permits are required under the Defence of the Realm Regulations are notified from time to time in the public press and by local notices, together with the regulations and conditions governing the issue of such Permits.

Use should be made of the Application Forms in this Book for all ordinary purposes under the following Regulations, of which copies can be seen at any Police Station :—

D.R.R. No.	Particulars of Application.
13	To be out of doors during hours prohibited under this regulation.
19	To photograph, sketch, &c., in an area prohibited under this regulation.
28, 29, 29B	To enter a specified place or area to which access has been prohibited or restricted under one or other of these regulations.

5. Before applying for a Permit for a particular purpose such as to enter a Special Military Area, or to sketch or photograph within an area prohibited for this purpose, you should complete the declaration of your identity on pages 2, 3, and 4, obtain the signatures of two male British-born householders, and read the further instructions at end.

(13148.) Wt. 30022—G 91. 100,000 Bks. 8/17, D & S. E 1486.

Permit Book   N⁰ 339756

DEFENCE OF THE REALM.

PERMIT BOOK.

☞ THIS BOOK MAY BE USED ONLY BY A BRITISH SUBJECT.

Anyone finding this book and unable to restore it to the person whose name and address are entered on page 1, must deliver it to an Officer of Police without delay.

This book should contain sixteen numbered pages in this cover, none of which must be removed.

[CROWN COPYRIGHT RESERVED.]

Harwich was one of the few restricted areas during the war and permit books were needed to enter parts of the town. The permit books had a photograph of the person and a description of them.

occupation, the visitor also had to state their nationality and length of visit. The forms had to then be given to the police. Local residents were issued with a pass containing their photograph if they needed to enter certain areas. As there were few visitors allowed into the town, the hotels mainly became redundant and were turned into hospitals.

The local population were informed that in the event of an enemy attack on the town they were to obey instructions from members of the local emergency committee and special constables.

In Grays the recruiting committee met at New Road School with Charles Seabrook presiding. The meeting was told that the Territorial Association at Grays was at deadlock as all the officers had been called away to other duties. The committee decided that it didn't need to do much recruiting but could deal with allowances for wives of those serving and liaise with the Soldiers' and Sailors' Families Association.

Dovercourt was close to the prohibited port of Harwich but still managed to get some visitors during the war.

As Christmas approached, there was an interesting offer for the volunteer entering the forces. Anyone who enlisted in the week before Christmas was to be given a holiday, with an advance of Army pay until after the Christmas period finished. This meant that they could still spend the festive season with their families. This was to encourage volunteers as numbers had fallen as the holiday period approached.

TWO

1915

The war had led to the Germans beginning a new form of attack unheard of in any previous conflict; Zeppelins began to bomb the towns and cities of England. Yarmouth and King's Lynn were bombed in January resulting in twenty deaths and numerous injuries. As well as bombing civilians, the Germans used poison gas for the first time against the Russians on the Eastern Front.

The Royal Navy began to enforce its superiority over the enemy upon the seas by blockading the German Navy in its homeports. They were less successful in trying to force their way through the Dardanelles.

April saw the beginning of the second Battle of Ypres during which the Germans used gas again. In the same month the ill-fated Anzac landing at Gallipoli took place.

May was an eventful month with the sinking of the *Lusitania* by a German U-boat resulting in 1,198 deaths and turning public opinion in many countries against the Germans. Italy entered the war on the Allied side and the Battle of Artois was fought to a standstill between the Germans and the French. At home the last purely Liberal government of Britain came to an end when Asquith formed an all-party coalition.

Despite the outcry against the Germans when they had used it, September saw the first use of poison gas by the British, with devastating result; unfortunately this was on British troops after the wind changed and blew the gas back onto their own lines. The new weapon, the tank, was tested for the first time.

October saw the death of British nurse Edith Cavell, shot by the Germans for helping Allied soldiers escape from Belgium. Cavell had treated German as well as Belgian wounded, but this and the intervention by the Americans made no difference to her sentence.

In December, Douglas Haig became the commander of the British forces. Shortly afterwards the withdrawal from Gallipoli began and carried on into the following month. The withdrawal was a much more successful affair than the invasion and the ensuing conflict had been.

The year did not start on a positive note for the Navy when HMS *Formidable* was sunk by a torpedo fired from the submarine *U 24* off Lyme Regis. The incident happened on New Year's Day and the evidence that war news travelled fast in some areas was shown by Robert Taylor Bull of Burnham who recorded the incident in his diary the following day. He noted that it blew up in the Channel and that only 150 of the crew survived. It seems that the news was not entirely accurate as in fact 199 survived from the crew of 750, but the early reports may have not known the final figures.

Essex played its part in aiding ships that were torpedoed at sea. Damaged ships were towed to Mucking Flats where they were beached. If possible, the ships were repaired and once more went into use in aid of the war effort. The ships were watched over by the boat of the Essex Coast Patrol. The boat they used could sail in shallower waters than most naval ships as they watched out for German submarines.

There was to be some level of evacuation of civilians from London into the Essex countryside to escape the bombing. Much of this was unofficial when children went to stay with relatives. There was also some movement of orphaned children into homes in the countryside. Orphans often stood out among the local population because of their better clothes and smarter appearance.

Many orphaned children found themselves in workhouses and in early 1915 there were over 7,000 children in workhouses in the country. There were attempts to get them out of these institutions by sending them to foster homes.

This was part of a wider move to get residents out of workhouses. Any able-bodied men were encouraged to take jobs in the growing workforce needed to

Orphan children often stood out because of their neat clothes and well cut hair. The girls at this establishment, the Dr Barnardo's home, look very smart.

Another view of the Dr Barnado's home for girls near Ilford. Tea is served on the lawn.

The Yeomanry were a common sight in pre-war Essex. They often held displays at fêtes and village fairs. Many lost their horses during the war and fought as infantry.

produce the goods for the war. There were even old soldiers in some workhouses who rejoined the Army once the war began. Unfortunately these old soldiers were often replaced by other wounded and discharged members of the forces who ended up in workhouse infirmaries.

The early arrival of the Zeppelins began to cause panic and rumours as early as January. A rumour started that two Zeppelins had been shot down over Chelmsford. It was also said that the airships had been circling the cathedral in Chelmsford but that the building had not received any damage owing to the power of prayer from those inside the building.

The mayor of East Ham was quoted in the newspapers as saying that it was astonishing how men could carry on taking out their girlfriends and sitting at home in front of the fire after what had happened to the civilian population in Belgium at the hands of the invading German Army. In his opinion they should have all enlisted by this time.

The mayor of East Ham's views could well have applied to another recruiting meeting held at Ilford Town Hall. The meeting was well attended but there was little enthusiasm for enlisting. Sir John Bethell MP, addressing the meeting, told the audience that if every man of military age came forward and enlisted, the war would be over very soon.

Some of the first soldiers sent across to the continent were now returning to the county, as the wounded men from France began to arrive back. The available hospitals could not cope and with the numbers and private houses, halls and even schools were taken over to house the wounded. The Middlesex

Ilford Town Hall was the venue for a recruitment meeting that wasn't very successful.

Convalescent Home in Holland Road, Clacton, was responsible for helping thousands of soldiers during the war. The Palace Hotel at Southend became the Queen Mary's Naval Hospital. Aveley School also became a hospital.

The Middlesex Convalescent Home at Clacton was another wartime hospital.

The Palace Hotel at Southend became a large hospital during the war. The wounded must have had lovely views over the sea.

The Married Quarters, Warley Barracks, near Brentwood.

A MERRY CHRISTMAS TO YOU

Married quarters in barracks during wartime were only for the regular soldiers' families. Volunteers and later conscripted men did not get the chance to move their families in.

Warley Barracks stood in a large forested area.

Treatment of the sick was not the only task that nurses had to deal with in the hospitals. For every man who arrived, long forms had to be completed within a certain time limit and sent to the War Office. When wounded men from the Colonial forces began to arrive the forms had to be duplicated and a copy sent to the headquarters of the relevant forces as well as the War Office.

New territorial nurses were given £8 to pay for their uniform and equipment. This included three dresses, indoor and outdoor capes, a bonnet and eating utensils. Many nurses bought drugs out of their own money for the men they were treating.

Treatment of the sick was not without risk for those who tried to help them. Private Rupert Blackmore of the 9th Lancers had an operation for appendicitis at Woolwich Hospital and was then sent to Fryerning Hall in Ingatestone to recuperate. The householder Alfred Rankin treated Blackmore like one of the family and gave him the run of the house. Blackmore then stole £17 14s 2d from the home. He was committed to trial with a recommendation for borstal training.

As well as the wounded in hospitals there were many who had recovered to some degree from their wounds but who could no longer serve at the front. It was not unusual to see the workforce of factories, coming out at the end of a shift, including a number of men with either an arm or a leg missing. Even then they were the lucky ones as a sight that was just as common was young women dressed in black, mourning their lost husbands. This seemed to be especially true in churches where many people who had not been regular worshippers suddenly began to attend; especially women grieving for lost husbands or sons.

Churches during the war were often grand buildings from an earlier period. They were often well attended and ran Sunday schools as well, like this one in Barking.

Cycling clubs were very popular at this time.

Whatever the results of the war and however visible they were, life in most local towns went on as before. The milkman would do his rounds on a horse and cart and carry a large can of milk up to the door of the houses. He would then use a pint or half-pint measure to pour the milk into the householder's own receptacle. The baker would also travel around the town by cart selling his bread and cakes.

Local farmers could also often be seen with a cartload of fruit and vegetables for sale. Another common sound was that of the 'pots and pans man' as he shouted his arrival in a cart covered with new pans and the offer to repair old ones.

Not everyone used horse and carts. The fish seller may have used a handbarrow. The muffin man would usually carry a try of his wares on his head rather than having his own transport.

Not all businesses were unhindered by the war however, as a complaint was made by the Revd Mr J.H. Pemberton concerning Hainault Forest School. He complained to the local corporation that the quality of the firewood supplied to the school was poor. It was, he claimed, now impossible to light a fire quickly with the wood supplied.

He was told that due to the war it was not possible to obtain the normal wood so other kinds had to be used to keep the industry going. The reverend was told that he didn't know how well off he was and that he could try to get wood somewhere else if he could. Being in Hainault Forest, getting wood would have seemed a small problem.

Other industries were also having problems. Lord Roberts had made an appeal for field glasses that were needed by the troops. It seems that most field glasses in

Cycling meetings were very popular as the large crowd at this pre-war Chelmsford meeting shows.

Parks were well used during wartime and concerts in Barking Park attracted crowds of thousands.

the country had come from German manufacturers. Although 18,000 pairs had been collected, more were needed.

Travelling in the county was still not as safe as it would seem to be, as was illustrated by a serious rail crash at Ilford in January. A local train had left Gidea Park station at 8.40 a.m. packed with workers on their way to the city. As it passed through Ilford station and moved onto the fast line to London the Clacton express hit it, slicing the train in half. The crash was witnessed by hundreds of waiting passengers on the station platforms. There were nine deaths and eighty injured. Local territorials helped with the rescue of the victims.

The expectation of air raids led to the sighting of several batteries of guns and anti-aircraft guns on the Thames. They were placed at Canvey Island, known as Dead Man's Battery, which was part of an improvement in the east coast defences.

There were also anti-aircraft guns at Coalhouse Fort. Although the fort had become obsolete as a defensive building it was still a useful base along with searchlights, a minefield in the river and restrictions on ships using the Thames. Checking the ships was done by men from a ship called *Champion* that was moored in the river. Soldiers were billeted in the fort and in tents around it.

Steamers were a popular form of travel especially on days out to the coast from London sailing up the Thames.

Although the Tilbury Ferry may be steam-powered, the other vessels on the river are still reliant on sail.

There was an interesting appeal in the *Essex Times* by a member of the Essex and Suffolk Royal Garrison Artillery based at the fort. He wrote a letter to the newspaper asking for help for himself and others among the 160 men based at Coalhouse. The letter stated that when the man's company had been mobilised in August 1914 they had been given a £5 bounty. They were then given another 10s for using the civilian articles that they had brought with them.

The letter then went on to list the equipment they were given: two pairs of boots, one shirt, one pair of socks, two pairs of pants, one jersey and a pair of gun floor shoes. They then had to use the bounty to buy more socks and shirts as they had only been given one. Some of the later recruits had not even been given the £5. Other companies had been given three pairs of boots, three pairs of socks, three shirts, towels, hair brushes and a holdall. The letter showed how the men enlisting were treated so differently when one would have expected that there was a uniform approach to the men joining the Army. The writer hoped that someone would read the letter and be able to do something about it.

Tilbury Fort also had a garrison and guns mounted. Soldiers were also stationed at the docks. The protection for the docks was provided by the Royal Dublin Fusiliers. A bridge was built across the Thames at Tilbury with a removable middle section to allow ships to pass through. The bridge stayed in place until October 1918. The fort itself was armed with anti-aircraft guns, which played a part in bringing down the Zeppelin *L 15*.

PICTURE PAVILION,

SOUTH STREET, ROMFORD.

Manager, FRANK COATES.   'Phone : ROMFORD 590.

Monday, Tuesday and Wednesday, March 8th, 9th & 10th,

Special Booking of the Most Exciting Society Drama,

GENTLEMAN CROOK

(IN THREE ACTS).

THIRD INSTALMENT of the Grand Serial Drama,

THE TREY O' HEARTS

(THE SEA VENTURE).

Thursday, Friday & Saturday, March 11th, 12th & 13th,

Exclusive Booking of the Most Sensational
Sporting Drama ever produced,

THE GREAT TURF SENSATION

(IN TWO ACTS).

Supported by an All-Round Star Programme.

Continuous Performance from 6 o'clock. Matinees, Wednesday and Saturday, at 2.30.

PRICES : 9d., 6d. and 3d.   CHILDREN, 6d., 4d. and 2d.
x182-33

There seem to have been some exciting films showing at Romford; no doubt they were well supported by the local troops.

At Purfleet, anti-aircraft guns were also mounted and 160 wooden huts were added to the barracks there for the new recruits. The huts were lined with boards to make them warmer. The boards came from the nearby Thames Paper Company. A large tented camp was also opened at nearby Belhus Park, Aveley, which was in place for the whole war.

As well as the huts for men to live in, a YMCA hut was also opened at the camp following a donation by the Cutlers Company. Lord Kinnaird came to the camp to make the presentation and open the new hut. During his speech he said that they had hoped to provide 200 huts at various camps and abroad but had by this time already opened 250. They hoped to reach 300 in the very near future.

The huts were there to provide healthy recreation for the men at the camp. The Reverend Norman Wright from Goodmayes was one of the chaplains at the camp. He praised the good work being done by the YMCA at Purfleet and elsewhere.

There were also a number of anti-aircraft guns inland. Pole Hill in Chingford had been used as a Scout and cadet camp by Vyvyan Richards, a teacher at Bancroft School. His friend T.E. Lawrence, later known as Lawrence of Arabia, was also involved in this camp and owned land there. During the war however, an anti-aircraft gun was set up on the site and the crew also grew vegetables in the fields nearby.

The lack of news of loved ones fighting in the war must have been hard to bear for those left at home. A letter printed in *The Times* in February from an

The policeman in the photograph must have had a busy time if one is to believe the number of crime reports in Barking in the local newspapers.

unnamed woman in Chelmsford pointed out one of the difficulties. She had not heard from her brother, who was in the Army, for some time. When she contacted other members of his battalion she was told that he had not been seen for some time and was believed to have been captured. She later found his name on a casualty list but it was wrongly spelt and his number was wrong. She asked that the War Office do what it could to be more forthcoming with information to the families of fighting men.

In February the police reported that there had been a drop in crime since the beginning of the war. The reasons given for this was that people were keeping better hours due to the darker streets, the early closing of public houses and a new idea of patriotism and duty. There was also lower unemployment and supposedly increased prosperity owing to more jobs, longer hours and the billeting of troops and the rent they paid of 9d a day. There was also a bigger market for food sales, which improved the lot of farm workers as well as those involved in industry.

The early air raids were carried out by Zeppelin and there was a raid in February. The majority of the bombs dropped seemed to have little effect, often falling on open fields. During this raid only five bombs were reported to have been dropped: one in Colchester, one in Coggeshall and three in Braintree.

At a meeting of the Braintree Urban Council on 22 February, officers from the 5th Notts & Derbyshire Regiment heard the chairman George Hunnable praise

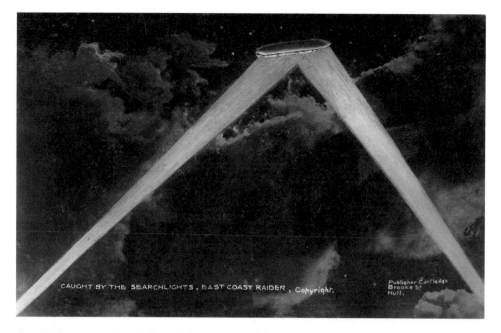

Searchlights were positioned along the Essex banks of the Thames and were used to pick out German airships.

The Zeppelin raids often caused more damage to property than they did to people. A headline in the Daily Mirror *concerning this raid on Colchester said, 'Sky pirates fail to kill a single baby.'*

the bravery of two of their members during the raid. Corporal Large and Private Goodall had found a bomb in a field and used a stick through the tail of the device to carry it to the river. They carried on walking with the bomb even after it burst into flames. Large was presented with a silver cigarette case and Goodall with a silver watch.

In March there was a change in the service conditions of the Anti-Aircraft Corps when the usual four-hour watch was changed to six hours. The men worked one day on, one day off. The changes led to protests from a number of professional people who were volunteers that they may not be able to manage to carry on with this work while following their profession. It seems that the AAC were almost entirely made up of volunteers from the professions. One crew was said to have two solicitors, a barrister and a musician in it.

There was also some criticism of the uniform of the corps. This was a blue lounge suit with a white naval cap and small red badges. The uniform was likened to that of a taxi driver or a railway porter.

It was not only the soldiers who were suffering from illness. Burnham School was stricken by an outbreak of measles in April. The illness was so bad that the Medical Officer closed the school down.

One illness to strike Essex was cerebro-spinal (spotted) fever. A warning by local government said that there must not be overcrowding in billets that allowed the disease to spread. There was also a warning issued for anyone who thought that he may have the disease against kissing, as this was one way to spread it.

During one raid in April, two women were witnesses to a strange event. The ladies were staying in a bungalow named the Hut near Latchingdon. They woke up to the sound of explosions. Then a car passed with its headlights shining on the road between Maldon and Burnham. The car was being followed by a Zeppelin. The report did not make clear whether the car was suspected of leading the Zeppelin or whether the airship was actually chasing it.

A report in the *Manchester Guardian* in April stated that although Zeppelins often bombed small places, such as they did in mid-April when they bombed Maldon and Heybridge, they often missed the larger, more important targets such as Harwich.

May was to be the month when several things occurred to turn British public opinion against their enemy (not that there needed to be many more reasons after the tales from Belgium). There had been a feeling among many members of the public, backed up by some politicians and several newspapers, that all enemy aliens present in Britain should be locked up. The debate on this topic had been going on since the war began.

Political meetings were regular events in those days as there was no other way for the politicians to get their views across to a public that did not own radios. Robert Taylor Bull did not only attend local meetings but in May he travelled up to London and attended a meeting at Kingsway Hall, at the West London Mission where he saw Lloyd George.

Not all meetings held were in support of the government or the aims of the war. The fact that people could speak against the government still during war is a

Another humorous card, but the examination being given by the nurse may have been a quite accurate portrayal of how thorough some medicals were.

sign that despite some abuses there was still free speech for most people. There was a meeting at East Ham Town Hall of the League of Rights for Soldiers' and Sailors' Wives. The speakers included Sylvia Pankhurst, Sir John Bethell MP and William Lansbury. The main complaint of those at the meeting was that the allowances given to the wives of the men serving in the Army were too low. Bethell obviously gave the government view and said that many MPs thought that allowances should be raised and that they eventually would. It seems strange that not all MPs held this view when one thinks of the sacrifice these men were making.

Miss Pankhurst said that the Soldiers' and Sailors' Families Association was the watchdog of the government rather than the friend of the soldier's wife. Lansbury said that women should band together and kick the government very hard.

There was an even greater feeling of revulsion against German nationals living in Britain to come, due to spy scares and other reasons with a sounder basis in fact. What was not known to the general public who were asking for the arrest of foreigners was that a special Intelligence Department had been founded in 1911 and that several suspicious aliens had been arrested and interned at the outbreak of war. Many others followed and those who were not interned were under severe restrictions and had to alert the police to any change of address.

One of the strangest examples of an alien breaking these regulations was Harry Landberg, an Austrian, who was arrested for not telling the police he had changed his address and who was then imprisoned for six months. The reason Harry had changed his address was that he was a member of the Essex Regiment and had moved to barracks in Colchester.

Another strange alien story was that of Fred Roberts who was a champion walker in Essex. Roberts worked at Wanstead Telephone Exchange as an inspector. He was charged at Stratford with failing to register as an Austrian. He had actually gone to a police station himself and said that until 1905 he had believed himself to be English. It was only in 1905 when he got his birth certificate, needed for his job, that he found out he had been born in Austria and his real name was Diegal. The telephone exchange had been taken over by the government and as they knew there that he was Austrian he did not feel as though he had to tell anyone else. The magistrate said his country was at war with Britain and that he could have intercepted important telephone messages. He was sent to prison for three months.

To add to the bad feeling that already existed against enemy aliens, on 7 May a German submarine torpedoed the *Lusitania*, a passenger ship with over 1,000 people on board. The *Manchester Guardian* printed an interview with one of the survivors; Edward Negus who came from Rickling in Essex and had been a second-class passenger on the ship. Negus claimed that two torpedoes had been fired at the ship. The first did the most damage, causing the ship to turn on its side and the second he believed hit the deck as the ship was turned over and the lifeboats were being lowered. Negus had been clinging to the rail that was above the water but fell off and slipped down the hull of the ship into the water as it turned over. He was pulled into a lifeboat by its sole occupant, a steward. They then went on to pick up fifty more people.

Any opportunity for portraying the Germans as monsters was eagerly jumped upon by the British press. When a commemorative medallion of the sinking of the *Lusitania* was pressed in Germany it was noticed that the medallion had the wrong date on it, saying 5 May. This was used as evidence that the Germans had in fact planned to sink the ship beforehand.

Reports from Germany seemed to show that the German public had little idea of how the action of sinking the *Lusitania* would be seen by the rest of the world. Public opinion in Germany seemed to be that the ship was carrying munitions and was therefore a legitimate target and that the sinking by submarine was actually an event to be proud of as it showed the power of the German Navy.

The sinking of the ship, as well as causing bad feeling, also led to the circulation of rumours. One of these was that a number of spies had been shot in Ireland where it was believed that some of the anti-British Irishmen were helping the Germans.

The portrayal of Germans as monsters who had no regard for the lives of innocent people was a popular theme of the newspapers at the time, both national and local. The newspapers also had a lot to say about the danger from enemy aliens present in this country. The real truth about what this scare-mongering resulted in was less well known. Many of the actions carried out by those responsible for dealing with enemy aliens would have not been out of place among the secret police of Russia.

It seems that any denunciation by any person against someone suspected of German sympathies would be investigated. This meant that anyone with a grudge against another person could denounce them, or anyone whose lifestyle may have been slightly removed from the norm could become a suspect. Some of the cases dealt with in Essex follow.

George Downing was previously a seaman but had settled at Parkstone and did a number of jobs at the local docks. He had married a German woman before the war and her parents had also moved in with them. Another factor in his supposed bad character was that he was a drinker. It was also believed that his wife had brothers in the German Army. Because the local population were averse to having Germans in their midst, the whole family was interned.

A Mrs Bellamy of Battlesbridge had a sister, Helen Gregory, who had worked before the war as a governess in Germany for fifteen years. Because she still received letters from Germany she was looked upon as suspicious and so was her sister who was also investigated.

A man named Heaseman of High Garret, Braintree, was suspected of having Germany sympathies. He did not associate or converse with local people but did often visit the Germans being kept at Southend.

Heavy drinking was, it seems, also looked upon as suspicious when it came to German sympathies. Harry Rome of Canvey Island was said to be under the influence of his German wife and to be a heavy drinker. When he heard about the explosion at Chatham in May 1915 he laughed in the faces of local inhabitants. He was recommended for expulsion from the local area.

Canvey Island was still sparsely populated during the war, although there were some gun batteries on the island.

Even a Roman Catholic children's home in Maldon came under suspicion. A letter was received from the War Office asking local officials if there were any German nuns at St Joseph's Home. Any German nuns had in fact been replaced by Dutch nuns and all the children in the home were British.

One of the worst cases was of a man named Frank Gourley, a member of the National Reserve and the postmaster at Tendring. His wife was German but they had one son serving in the British Navy and another serving in the Suffolk Regiment. A soldier supposedly alleged that Mrs Gourley had German sympathies. An agent was then sent to approach her acting as a German sympathiser but received no encouragement. Despite this Mrs Gourley was relieved of her postmistress job and the family were then ordered to leave the area.

Danger to the war effort did not only come from enemy aliens it seemed. Vandalism seems to be a modern phenomenon according to most people, but this obviously is far from the truth. At one sitting at East Ham magistrate's court in April, ten young boys were charged with wilful damage and theft. Five of the boys were charged with wilful damage to the London and North West Railway coal depot at Plashet Lane, Upton Park. The boys released the brakes on a number of coal trucks causing them to run down the track and crash into a gate. If the gate had not held the trucks could have ended up on the mainline. There was obviously no protection of the names of juveniles in those days as all the boys' names were printed in the *Essex Times*. They were fined 2s 6d each.

Three eleven-year-olds were charged with stealing chocolate from a shop. Of these one boy had already been birched and he was sentenced to five lashes. The other two got probation. Two other boys were charged with stealing bananas and also got probation.

There were continued reports in the press of Allied prisoners of war being badly treated in Germany. Although treatment of prisoners varied from camp to camp, the number of complaints would seem to point to some basis of truth for the claims. The fair treatment of German prisoners then upset some members of the public who thought they were being treated too well. Then of course air raids on civilians was perhaps the worst thing that could have happened for enemy aliens in Britain.

Another problem with identifying enemy aliens was that there was no real national system of identification. Passports were rare up to the war and were not needed to travel in Europe. There were several systems of identifying people but none that were nationally organised until 1915. There was a national registration of the population and identity cards were issued which included the holder's nationality. This seems to have been mainly used to identify men of military service age as once conscription began the ID cards had served their purpose and were mainly forgotten about.

In Essex, Southend was to suffer from a number of war-related incidents during the month of May. On the 10th there was an air raid by a Zeppelin. This was reported in *The Times* where it stated that the 'German lust for murder' led to the dropping of a hundred bombs, which killed one woman, a Mrs Whitewell of 120 North Road, Prittlewell. Mrs Whitewell was aged sixty and had been a member of the Salvation Army for forty years. The raid also caused £20,000 worth of damage.

The sinking of the *Lusitania* and the air raids seemed to be the sparks to set off the powder keg of ill-feeling and there were riots in several parts of the country during which German nationals were attacked and their property damaged. In Liverpool £40,000 worth of damage was done and 200 premises were gutted. There were also riots in Manchester and Newcastle as well as in parts of London.

The Southend air raid no doubt had some influence on events in the town a few days later. Although many of the foreigners in Britain had lived in the country for years and posed no threat, the outbreak of air raids and the use of U-boats by the Germans had influenced public opinion against them. Whether the people involved in attacks believed that these people really were a threat or that they were used a scapegoats is debatable.

The local newspaper the *Southend and Westcliff Graphic* did little to help calm public fears when they stated that any person with German blood should be considered a dangerous enemy. What occurred in the town was called in *The Times* a protest against German residents left at liberty.

Riots began in Southend and the mob wrecked premises in Queen's Road. The local Army commander called out all the troops in the area to assist the police in restoring order. Even this was not enough and two hundred special constables were

Southend suffered from a number of air raids during the war by Zeppelin and aeroplane. Perhaps the pier made the town visible to the enemy.

also brought in. The crowds were driven onto the High Street but still continued to attack premises.

There would seem to have been some sympathy with the views of the rioters shown by the authorities as only two arrests were made. The riots and attacks on foreigners were instrumental in the government finally deciding to intern foreign nationals and led to the creation of numerous large camps around the country.

As well as the camps, the confinement of foreigners also included prison ships moored in the Thames off Southend Pier. The *Royal Edward* and the *Ivernia* were liners and made quite pleasant prisons for those on board. They held 1,400 and 1,600 prisoners respectively. Ships were often more comfortable than camps as the cabins on ships were much easier to heat than drafty wooden huts.

At Stratford a clearing house was opened for internees who were later sent to permanent camps. As the internees were led through the town to the station on their way to permanent camps, crowds gathered, threw things, spat on them and called them baby killers.

There were also demonstrations against what was thought to be a German business in Grays. Hundreds of people gathered outside a furniture shop in the High Street. A representative of the shop came out and explained to the crowd that the owners had no German connections at all. In some places men with foreign-sounding names placed advertisements in local newspapers to explain that their name was not of German origin.

The people who were interned or who came to be seen as enemy aliens were often not that at all. A man named Gustav Pagenstecher had come to England in 1869 as the tutor to the Gurney family. The family were related to the prison reformer Elizabeth Fry. Pagenstecher did much to make sure that part of the Gurney estate in West Ham was not built on and survived, and still does today as West Ham Park. From 1914 until his death in 1916 however he was classed as an enemy alien and had to report to the police on a regular basis.

The air raids did not stop, however, and towards the end of the month a further two women died in another raid on Southend. The government advised householders to take out insurance policies against damage from air raids. There were no air raid sirens to warn of attacks at first. Warnings would sometimes be given by a police constable on a bicycle, riding around blowing a whistle with a sign around his neck saying take cover. Another form of air raid warning was a boy scout playing his bugle on street corners.

Some areas did have sirens later in the war. Romford had a siren on the chimney of the police station. Unlike during the Second World War there were no air raid shelters and most people would sit under the table as a means of protection. As the main form of light was oil lamps or candles and heating was by coal fire, these would often be put out in case of bomb damage, which then led to fire. Many therefore sat through air raids in the dark.

It seems that it was not only German airships that were to be feared. A naval balloon managed to break free near Grays throwing the officer in charge of it into the Thames, luckily only into a shallow part of the river. The balloon had a grappling hook attached and as it floated across the area it crossed the causeway of the training ship *Exmouth* and caught Henry Curtiss, the officer of the watch, cutting his left arm and hand. The balloon was eventually brought back under control by the officers from the *Exmouth*.

In response to the threat from the air, airfields were opened in several parts of Essex. There had been pre-war airfields in the county, at Dagenham, Barking and Fairlop. Another early airfield had been at Chingford Marshes and this was opened as a Royal Naval Air Station in May. A number of local men gained their flying certificates at the site. One of the men based there was Ivor Novello who wrote 'Keep The Home Fires Burning'. The song was supposedly sung by the airmen on numerous occasions in the nearby King's Head public house.

The arrival of troops in the county did not stop as the war went on. More schools became billets for soldiers. In some schools which did stay open the number of refugees arriving led to half-day teaching with locals taught in the morning and newcomers in the afternoon.

The position of schools varied from area to area. As early as 1914 the government had said that children should be allowed to help out at harvest time and many children did just this. There was also the problem of school staff enlisting which meant a shortage of teachers. When the father of the family left home to fight, the older children often had to leave school to work or help out at home.

Barking was similar to many towns in Essex with a built up town centre surrounded by small rural groups of houses.

In some schools the children dug up the playgrounds to grow vegetables. Children were also set tasks to do such as collecting conkers. This had some connection with munitions but I'm not sure in what capacity. They also collected fruit to make jam. Children also sewed or knitted at school to make items for the troops and even wound rolls of bandages. The Essex Education Committee meeting in July discussed the possibility of teaching pupils how to milk cows and do other farm work in schools so that children would be better workers on farms.

In Colchester the council did as much as possible to welcome the new military arrivals by producing a local guide for soldiers. In this guide it listed the thirty-seven clubs for servicemen and, in some cases, their wives. At these clubs the men could get cheap refreshments, recreation, reading and writing materials and at some baths and laundry services. There were even French lessons available to prepare them for the day when the men would go abroad.

Although the war was obviously taking away the majority of young men, those who were left did still manage to have some lighter moments. There were still people going on holiday in the summer months. Although paid holidays were rare for most workers, even working class people could often manage a cheap day trip to the seaside. During 1914 holidaymakers seemed to be heading for either the south or west coasts as the east coast including Essex was the one nearest the enemy and therefore more at risk. By the summer of 1915 however, things seemed to have changed and, according to a report in *The Times*, the thrill of Zeppelin raids were in fact a lure in attracting more adventurous people to the east for their holidays.

The trains to the east from London during the war were smaller and were infrequent so those that did run in the summer months were very crowded. *The Times* gave the reasons for going east as habit, because that was where the holidaymakers always went or to visit soldiers who were stationed there. Most of the holidaymakers were women and children. Some went with the hope of seeing either a Zeppelin or somewhere that had been attacked by one.

No doubt there were two main resorts that the majority of the holidaymakers headed for. Southend had been growing in popularity as a resort for Londoners since the mid-nineteenth century. The pier was a great attraction and for those who did not want to brave the crowded trains there were always the steamboats that travelled from London to deposit their load at the end of the pier. The Kursaal had also been a great attraction since it opened in 1901. The whole place was full of rides and amusements that drew in the day-tripper. It was also at times a billet for soldiers and the population of Shoeburyness.

Clacton had also been growing in popularity since the late nineteenth century and, although its pier was nowhere near the same length as the one at Southend, it was still an attraction; an attraction no doubt added to by the entertainment provided by men such as Professor George Webb who would ride a bicycle off the end of the pier or jump off in a blazing sack. However, when the pier was mined during the war there was less inclination for holidaymakers to venture on it.

The arrivals at new barracks were not all faceless strangers. At Grey Towers in Hornchurch the 1st Sportsman's Battalion moved into the new camp. Many of them were well known people from the worlds of sport and entertainment. At Hare Hall Camp in Romford more celebrities had moved in with the 2nd Sportsman's Battalion.

There was one soldier who was to get to know Hare Hall Camp well. He was first there as a member of the Sportsman's Battalion as a private and then returned as a trainee officer with the Artist Rifles who later took over the camp. Far from being a rough person that the locals may have to worry about (as many of the soldiers were), W.S. Ferrie was a minister in the United Free Church in Scotland. He described how the men in his unit would often walk into Romford during the evenings and would be invited to visit places of interest such as the brewery.

Ferrie also became very involved in local religion and would preach to both his fellow soldiers and the locals at the Congregational Church in Romford. He may have even been the first person to comment on the supposedly loose morals of Essex girls as he mentioned that the behaviour of the girls in Romford was cheap and that this made the men who associated with them cheap as well.

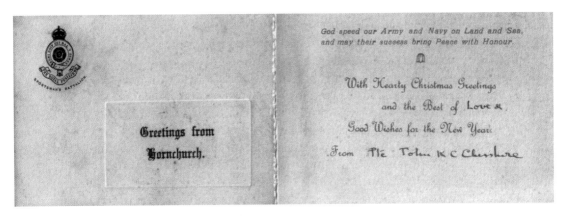

A Christmas card sent by a member of the Sportsman's Battalion from Grey Towers Camp at Hornchurch.

Some members of the artillery based at Coalhouse Fort were not happy with the equipment they were provided with and wrote to the Essex Times to complain.

The Sportsman's Battalion were replaced at Hare Hall Camp with the Artist Rifles, which had by this time become an officer training corps. They were an elite regiment shown by the fact that recruits had to pay to join, as did the sportsmen. The Artists paid £1 5s, a large amount in those times and this would have deterred the average working man from becoming a member.

Included in the Artists at Romford were some of the better-known war poets such as Edward Thomas, many of whose poems had a local content. He mentioned Childerditch, Pyrgo, Wingle Tye and Margaretting in his poems among other places in Essex. In her book about her husband, Helen Thomas described how he loved the route marches in the county and although he had not known Essex before, he found it beautiful and moving. Helen and their children had moved to a cottage in Epping Forest at one point to be near her husband when he was based at High Beech.

An unusual naval disaster took place in June. It was unusual because it was on land. Damage valued at £12,000 was caused by a fire at a cork lifebelt factory at Barking Wharf. The factory, machinery and a large amount of stock were destroyed.

There was a mysterious event in July when the Germans reported that Harwich had been bombed and that there had been damage to Landguard Fort on the Suffolk side of the river and to the destroyers based in the harbour. There

Summer Foliage, Epping Forest, near High Beech.

One of the war poets, Edward Thomas, moved his family to a cottage in Epping Forest so they could be near him while he was based at High Beech.

Tilbury Fort was another ancient defensive structure that played a part in the war.

was no report of this attack happening in the British press. It was stated that German radio broadcasts that were false were censored. The broadcast about Harwich was not censored so would, in that case, seem to have been correct. If it was then why was it not reported?

In August the *Princess Juliana* docked at Tilbury carrying 258 wounded British servicemen. They had been released by the Germans as being unfit for further duty. They were greeted by a large crowd and a band. The report of the arrival in *The Times* stated that the men had been badly mistreated by the Germans in that they had not only been starved but that many had been the victims of violence by their captors.

Stories of German mistreatment of British prisoners were rife during the war. They were often used as an argument for being less considerate to the German prisoners being held in Britain who were seen as being treated too leniently.

There were still some unusual crimes tried in court; in August, Grace Shepard of Stock sued Frank Jarvis, a builder also of Stock, for breach of promise. Miss Shepard was awarded £600 damages, a large amount for that time.

A deserter from the Royal Fortress Artillery based at Woolwich was sentenced to six months' imprisonment at Clerkenwell in September. Thomas Baker had been impersonating Corporal John Smyrk of the 2nd Essex Regiment who at the time was a prisoner of war in Germany. Baker had been so successful in his deception that he had even been staying with relatives of Smyrk's girlfriend.

The Essex Education Committee meeting in September approved the formation of Cadet Corps for boys in all elementary schools in Essex. As soon as the boys left school they could join. These cadet forces would be part of the territorials and would give the boys some military training before they reached the age to enlist in the regular Army. It seems that Essex was the first county to do this and hoped that their example would be followed by others.

Another crime that became common during the war but that had not been happening before was showing a light. There was a partial blackout in force and in Colchester Paul Summers of Crouch Street was charged with the offence after being arrested by a special constable. He was given a choice: pay a 30s fine or face fourteen days' imprisonment.

Travel in the county was still a problem and this meant that it was not always possible for troops to move around easily. Although much development of amenities, apart from the growth of Army camps, slowed down during the war, there was some upgrading of roadways. A new bridge was opened on Southend Road at Wickford. The road to Tilbury Fort was also improved to make access to the fort and docks easier.

Although those working in munitions were doing long hours, there must also have been some leisure time associated with their work. In September a charabanc carrying thirty workers from a munitions factory at Enfield was on its way to Cambridge on a works outing. As it climbed Woodredon Hill between Waltham Abbey and Epping it began to run backwards down the hill and the brakes failed. Two of the passengers jumped out; one died and the other was seriously injured. The driver managed to pull the vehicle across the road and stop it against the bank. The rest of the passengers only suffered slight injuries.

There were air raids on Colchester in September and during one raid on the 14th, five Zeppelins hovered over the town for two hours. As soon as notification of a raid was received, the police and the specials made sure that all the lights were out. All trams and other traffic was stopped and watchers from the tower of the town hall made sure that no lights were showing in the town.

Another new crime came to the attention of the public in November. Edward Rossiter of Essex was found guilty of burning down his bungalow with intent to defraud his insurance company. He claimed that the fire was started by a bomb. It seems however that there were no enemy planes in the area on the night in question. Mr Rossiter's comeuppance was that he was sentenced to six months' hard labour.

A Mr Miller Christy from Chignal St James near Chelmsford kept detailed notes of the sound of gunfire from Flanders that could be heard from his home. The levels of sound depended on wind direction and he wrote articles for the *Journal of the Meteorological Society*. He said that the loudest noise was on 11 September.

"SPOTTED."
THE ZEPP RAIDER.
Passed for publication, by Press Bureau.

Another Zeppelin caught in the spotlight beams.

A large shopping parade for the period at Leigh-on-Sea.

The old pump at Prittlewell. Many homes in rural Essex still did not have a water supply and the population relied on public pumps.

Band concerts were a popular form of entertainment as the number of seats surrounding this bandstand at Westcliff shows.

The fear of air raids did not stop people visiting places like Southend. A report in The Times *suggested that the chance of seeing an air raid might have been one of the attractions.*

Despite the large number of volunteers who rushed to enlist when the war began, there were still shortages of men towards the end of 1915. The encouragement of recruits was delegated to local levels and in Clacton Lord Derby was organising a campaign to canvass local men who had yet to join the Army. Letters were sent out directing canvassers to enlist as many local men as possible.

The canvassers were given leaflets containing a list of questions that possible recruits often asked when approached to join. It seems that one of these commonly asked was would married men have to go and fight while single men were still not in the Army. Lord Derby's response was that everything that could be done to encourage single men to go first was being done.

THREE

1916

There was a significant breakthrough in medical treatment in 1916 when the Royal Army Medical Corps carried out their first successful non-direct blood transfusion. This would obviously make a great deal of difference to the treatment of the wounded in some places, although not of course in the basic emergency stations close to the front. The progress of the war was less successful with the withdrawal from Gallipoli still underway. Elsewhere, Paris was bombed by Zeppelins for the first time.

This was to be the year of the great battles, which were expensive in terms of lives lost and were to gain little ground for either side. It began in February when the Germans attacked the French at Verdun. It was an attack that was to go on for ten months with each side losing more than 300,000 men.

April saw the heaviest gas attack of the war so far by the Germans at the Battle of Hulluch. The Easter Rising in Ireland gave the government serious military problems to deal with nearer home. There were serious outbreaks of violence in Dublin where it took six days for the British forces to regain order.

The end of May and early June saw the Battle of Jutland, one of the largest naval battles of the war, involving 250 ships and which ended in stalemate. Fourteen British ships were sunk and eleven German. Later in the same month a further naval disaster saw the sinking of the HMS *Hampshire*, which struck a mine and sunk. The sinking also had serious consequences for the Army. It led to the death of one of the ship's passengers, Lord Kitchener, who had been on a trip to Russia to try and persuade the Czar to continue the war against the Germans.

The Battle of Verdun between the French and the Germans was one of the reasons that led to the British attack on the Somme in July as a means of taking some pressure off the French. The battle was a disaster with many of the new volunteer regiments being decimated during worthless attacks that gained no more than a few yards. In this conflict any ground made was often soon lost again. There were 60,000 allied casualties on the first day. The 'Pals' battalions, mainly from northern England, were so badly decimated that whole streets or even towns lost the majority of their young men on the same day. The battle also

The first tanks were successful in frightening the German soldiers. Unfortunately the mechanical working of the new machines were not as successful and they often broke down.

saw the first use of tanks by the British. Although the weapon was a great success when it worked, mechanical unreliability meant that success was rare.

November finally saw the end of the Battle of the Somme as the bad weather set in.

The following month David Lloyd George became Prime Minister of Britain and the new fighter plane, the Sopwith Camel, was introduced.

There were several reports in the local newspapers about the events that had occurred in workhouses at Christmas. Chelmsford Workhouse held 220 people at the time, which a report was quick to point out included no able-bodied men. The workhouse was decorated for the Christmas celebrations.

In Billericay Workhouse the inmates were given roast pork and plum pudding. The men received an ounce of tobacco and a pipe as a gift and the women were each given sweets, nuts and an orange. Whether the reports were a true representation of conditions in these institutions is another matter.

Christmas dinners were obviously worthy of news either for workhouse inmates or soldiers as the *Essex County Standard* had a report on the Christmas meal of the Essex Regiment based at Harwich. It consisted of pork, beef, chicken, mince pies, plum pudding and beer. There were obviously no worries about food shortages at that time. The report also mentioned that while the Essex Regiment had their dinners in huts, the Essex and Suffolk Royal Garrison Artillery, who were manning the guns at Harwich, had theirs at the drill hall.

There was a meeting at Earlham Hall in Forest Gate early in January to discuss the Belgian refugees living in the area. Two houses had been made available for the refugees. No. 4 Norwich Road and no. 20 St Georges Road had been given by their owners to the organisation dealing with the refugees. It was reported to the meeting that all the male refugees were now working which had removed the financial burden from them but that none of the men were of war service age.

Despite the huge numbers of men who had already gone overseas, the billeting of troops was still a problem in the county. When the Surrey Yeomanry arrived in Ardleigh at one house, ten men slept on the kitchen floor. If the stay was to be longer than a day or two then the Army supplied the householder with beds for the men, although ten beds in the kitchen may have been difficult for the household to cope with. The men were also supplied with their own food while billeted in private homes. Families often became friendly with the men billeted in their homes and kept in touch with them when they went abroad.

Some families seemed to do more than others for the war effort. The Davies family of King's Road, East Ham, was one such example. The father of the family, William Davies, was serving with the National Reserve at Chelmsford. The three eldest sons, Charles, Bert and Fred were all serving with the 13th Battalion the Essex Regiment. The other son William was in the Royal Field Artillery. Two daughters were also serving with the 10th Essex Volunteers nurses. According to the local newspaper the family received a letter from the king praising their service to the country. Actually the letter was from Frederick Ponsonby, the Keeper of the Privy Purse, who had been told to write to them by the king.

Despite the excellent show put up by the Davies family, other people in East Ham were not so impressed with the quality of the local male population. The Revd Mr Thomas at East Ham Church praised the parade of Boy Scouts who attended a service there. He said that the Boy Scouts organisation gave its members discipline. He believed that twentieth-century boys lacked the grit and determination of their forefathers who had built the British Empire. Modern boys had too much luxury and had too much done for them by the state.

This was a rather surprising view when one considers the number of young men who had volunteered to go and fight. The reverend's view relating to state intervention was not an opinion that seemed to be shared by others; especially the wounded men returning from the Army and trying to get a pension from the state.

Hornchurch welcomed the arrival of 1,000 soldiers from New Zealand, all of them seriously wounded. Grey Towers Camp, previously occupied by the Sportsman's Battalion, became a hospital for the New Zealanders. The men included several Maoris from the Maori Battalion, which had been fighting at Gallipoli.

Grey Towers house was the site of the Sportsman's camp. It was described in the press as a fine old stately home of England. In fact it was less than fifty years old.

The Sportsman's Battalion aroused a lot of public interest in the media of the time due to their famous members and their physical size; many were over 6ft tall. They were given the nickname the 'Hard as Nails Battalion'.

The 2nd Sportsman's Battalion were based at Hare Hall Camp in Romford.

The local press did their bit to make the troops welcome in the county. The *Essex County Standard* printed a photograph of soldiers boarding a bus. The men were from the Notts & Derby Regiment, Sherwood Foresters, and were leaving West Mersea on leave. One of the men had an 'X' marked above his head and the headline stated that a box of cigarettes was waiting for the marked man if he came to the newspaper's offices.

Crime was still in evidence in the county and violence towards women seemed to be quite a normal event. William Rose, a coal carter of Walton, was found drunk and disorderly. His wife and daughter had sought protection from him from the police.

There were also opportunities for crime that had not been in existence before the war. James O'Connor was described as a sergeant in the Royal Garrison Artillery but appeared in court charged with being an absentee. He was also charged with obtaining 1s and 2s by false pretences. O'Connor had approached a Mrs Fanny Curington and Mrs Margaret Smith at their homes posing as a billeting officer. When they agreed to take in soldiers he borrowed 1s from one of them and 2s from the other to pay for a telegram to be sent to his depot to fetch the soldiers.

Training for war could often be as dangerous as war itself and three members of the Irish Guards died in an accident at Warley Barracks. It was reported in the *Barking, Ilford & East Ham Advertiser* that a rifle grenade exploded as it was fired rather than when it landed. A fuller explanation was given in the *Manchester Guardian*. It seems that the grenade was fired but did not explode on hitting the ground. It was then put back on a rifle to fire it again and this time it did explode on firing.

Although three men died and the officer in charge and several non-commissioned officers were also hurt, the man who fired the rifle was, amazingly, uninjured.

Being proud of the men stationed in their area did not stop some locals from making a little extra money from the new arrivals. One soldier said that it was not unusual for a shopkeeper to charge 6d for a pair of shoelaces that a local only paid 3d for. An increase in business must have been welcome for local shopkeepers, especially in smaller towns and villages where the population at times doubled.

There was another reported case of breach of promise, this time at Grays. Lily Green accused Stanley Moore, who did not turn up in court to hear the case. Unlike the previous case in which damages were £600, this time they were only £25. It seems that it was not the serious level of the crime but the ability to pay that decided the amount of the damages.

The local nobility also did their bit in the conflict and Lady Petrie started a milking school at Thorndon Hall her country home at Brentwood. In all eighty-five children attended the school and went on to help out at local farms. The report did not say if Lady Petrie was involved in the milking lessons herself.

In March the Zeppelin *L15* bombed the village of Wennington. There was little damage as the incendiaries fell mainly in a field. There had been a cash prize offered for the first person to bring down a Zeppelin. The £500 prize was put up by Sir Charles Wakefield, the Lord Mayor of London.

The *L15* was commanded by Kapitän Breithaupt and it flew over Essex as one of a group of Zeppelins in March 1916. It was fired on by a number of anti-aircraft batteries along both banks of the Thames, including the one at Purfleet. The Zeppelin eventually crashed into the Thames Estuary.

The gunners at Purfleet believed they were responsible for bringing down the airship and so Captain J. Harris from Purfleet claimed the cash prize from the mayor. The War Office, however, decided that the Army could not accept the prize. They also agreed that the bringing down of the airship had been a joint action between Purfleet, Abbey Wood and Erith anti-aircraft guns.

Instead of the money, each man at Purfleet involved in the action received a gold medal with the name Sir Charles Wakefield on one side and a 3in gun and the date of the event on the other. No doubt the money would have been more welcome to those with families to support.

In a further connection with that night it was reported in *The Times* in October 1916 that 2nd Lt Alfred de Bathe Brandon of the Royal Flying Corps was awarded a DSO for gallant conduct. Brandon was a New Zealander who had studied at Cambridge and qualified as a barrister. Part of his award for gallant conduct included dropping a number of bombs on an airship on the night of 31 March 1916 while his aircraft was riddled with machine gun bullets from the Zeppelins. This all occurred while he was stationed at Hainault.

In April a Zeppelin hovered above Maldon Workhouse and used its own searchlight to pinpoint targets in the town. Twenty bombs were dropped. There were complaints by the residents that there was no attack on the airship from anti-aircraft guns or aircraft. The airship would have seemed to have been an obvious target while using a searchlight.

Grays Park was another of the well-used and popular public amenities that were becoming more common in Essex towns.

Japanese Pagoda, Palace by the Sea, Clacton-on-Sea.

The Japanese Pagoda, a popular attraction at Clacton.

Another problem caused by air raids was greater demand for telephones. Although still rare, those who did have private telephones often used them to call the police or someone else to tell them that there was a raid on. The use of telephones during raids was frowned upon by official sources as it delayed important messages getting through from the authorities. Individuals were urged not to use telephones during raids otherwise regulations would have to be introduced to restrict their use.

It was not only the air raids that posed a threat during the evening and night. In Barking, Mr James Bones of Westbury Road was killed by a bus that hit him in the dark. The driver reported that he did not see Mr Bones. It seems that the blackout may have saved lives from air raids but at the same time put civilians in danger on the dark roads.

The Battle of Jutland at the end of May had a local connection through a young boy named John Cornwell. John came from Leyton but had moved to Manor Park in 1910 when he was aged ten. He was a member of the Ilford Boy Scouts before joining the Navy. He was serving as a Boy First Class on HMS *Chester* and was wounded during the battle and subsequently died of his wounds.

John was originally buried at Grimsby but after being awarded the Victoria Cross his body was exhumed and he was given a state funeral with his coffin being pulled on a gun carriage from East Ham Town Hall to Manor Park Cemetery. Boy Scouts lined the route. A fund was started by the Mayor of East Ham which led to the building of six cottages in Hornchurch. A memorial plaque to John Cornwell is still there on the gatepost leading into the cottages.

There was an interesting court case in Brentwood that showed the change in finances that families could experience when the husband enlisted. Edna Green of Cromwell Road, South Weald, was charged with neglecting her five children. Before her husband had enlisted, his wages were between 20 and 24s a week. From this he gave his wife 10s to keep the home. While he was serving in the Army, his wife received 20s a week separation allowance meaning she was much better off.

This did not seem to help her children however, who were described by an NSPCC officer as 'verminous'. They had no proper beds to sleep in and very little bedding. They lived in two rooms but the children were often out in the street late at night as their mother was not at home. Soldiers often called at the house and stayed for hours. Mrs Green was sent to prison for three months.

Keeping older children off school to go to work was frowned upon by the authorities. Emily Rix of Chivers Road, Chingford, tried to get round this problem by changing the date on her daughter's birth certificate to show that she was a year older. She then blamed the alteration on her daughter. She was fined 20s.

The arrival of troops from other parts of the country must have been unusual enough in many of the smaller Essex villages where strangers were rare. The reaction in Hornchurch when the troops from New Zealand arrived must have been one of amazement. By this time even more men had come to join the first 1,000 who had arrived earlier in the year. How strange the new arrivals must have looked when some of them were Maoris who had been fighting the Turks in Gallipoli. In March the Maoris performed the haka for the locals at the drill hall in the village. There were twenty warriors in war paint and native costume. What the locals must have thought of it can only be imagined. This was in the days before the haka was a common sight performed on television before rugby matches. The majority of the population had probably never even seen a foreigner before this.

The local weather obviously did not agree with the Maoris and many suffered from chest complaints, including Prince Moki who was the son of the chief of the island of Niue. Although he was in the Maori Battalion he was actually Polynesian. He sadly died at Hornchurch of pneumonia. There are other Maoris buried in the churchyard at Hornchurch and although they have the same standard gravestones as others who died in the war, there is something that is most unusual about the Maori headstones. They have two names on them. I have never been able to find out any reason for this but it would seem to be related to their race as none of the other war graves in the cemetery, and there are many, have more than one name on them.

Despite the war, visits to the seaside did not stop completely. Because of the danger of invasion the coasts were defended. A postcard sent from Leigh-on-Sea by one holidaymaker mentioned that the area was full of soldiers and that there were trenches all along the seafront as defences against invasion.

A meeting of the town council at Romford heard that the local air raid committee needed another stretcher to be kept at the fire station at Hare Street. Perhaps this was related to the Army camps in the area, which would no doubt

The gravestones of Privates Vasau, Moki. Taleva and Filiqua. Two names on one gravestone for war dead is unheard of. There are two examples of this in Hornchurch, both for Maoris.

Away from the market place, Romford was much more of a normal shopping centre.

be a likely target for air raids. Twelve brown blankets, four first aid haversacks, six lamps and more bandages and splints were also needed. The Essex Volunteer Regiment agreed to act as stretcher-bearers during raids. The council also discussed the running of a bus service in the area. They were told that it would cost around £2,000 to bring the local roads up to a high enough standard for a bus. They decided to put the decision off until the following year.

Until now the British Army had always consisted of volunteers and still was in the early years of the war despite both the enemy and allied armies having conscription. The debate concerning conscription in Britain had been a long and well-argued one, but eventually conscription began in July for those aged between eighteen and forty-one.

There then began the tribunals, which sat to decide if a man had to serve in the forces or would be excused because of his occupation or for other reasons. The Halstead tribunal decided that workers on farms where there were more than three men employed to each 100 acres should serve in the forces. Rochford tribunal, however, seemed to believe that most farmhands should be exempt owing to the need to grow food for the country. This was especially applied to horsemen; the job was described as one of the most difficult to fill. The view of the tribunals and their decisions seemed to be influenced by local peculiarities.

Billericay tribunal seemed very lenient when they excused a baker, as he had to look after his mother, because there was no one else to do it. He was also running another business for a man who had already enlisted. Meanwhile at Southend tribunal, fifteen members of the fire brigade were forced to enlist despite the danger from fires due to air raids.

The opening hours of public houses were cut once again to stop those working in industry from spending all the extra money they made from overtime on drink.

A view of Leigh-on-Sea from the sea. Restrictions were placed on boats using the River Thames later in the war.

Westcliff was not commercialised at the time of the war, but had a large beach and bathing machines.

Ilford was another town to have a large well-kept park for the pleasure of the local inhabitants.

Ilford was a busy town in 1916 and yet there are a lack of men in uniform visible in this photograph.

There seemed to be a connection between drink and bad behaviour in Romford when four wooden posts were broken down in an alley next to the White Hart Inn. The posts were there to stop cycling in the alley and it was believed that the damage was done by soldiers.

In South Ockendon a farm colony owned by West Ham Council was taken over by the Army and became a large tented camp for new recruits. As with other camps it changed its use and later became a prisoner of war camp. The inmates of the POW camp later became a useful local workforce when labour was short.

There were ever-growing numbers of wounded men appearing in the county as the war went on. This was having an adverse effect on local services. Tilbury Cottage Hospital had a financial deficit of £145 for the previous year. This was due to the war and a record number of patients entering the hospital. The establishment did receive a subscription of £60 from the Port of London Authority and £52 from Grays Council, but even this did not lead to financial stability.

One of the main complaints concerning the way men who were invalided out of the Army through ill health were treated was the problem they had securing a pension. One explanation for this was given by William Dalton the honorary secretary of the Warley branch of the Soldiers' and Sailors' Families Association. He did not blame the pensions office but the Army Medical Board who passed men as fit to serve who were obviously not.

Dalton gave two examples. One was a man who suffered from varicose veins and who had spent much of his time in the Army in hospital. When he was demobbed he was refused a pension as he had suffered from the condition before joining up and it was not due to his service. Surely then he should not have been passed fit in the first place.

Another man failed his original Army medical as his chest measurement was insufficient and he was generally unfit. It seems that those who failed medicals had to take another two weeks later. Obviously this time the medical board were less stringent as he was passed as fit to serve in a garrison abroad. Dalton explained how the man was so ill that he collapsed while speaking to him.

In September, a Dr Armstrong-Jones retired from the mental hospital at Claybury. It was the first asylum built by the London County Council in the late nineteenth century. The grounds consisted of 300 acres of high ground overlooking Epping Forest and were large enough for over 2,000 patients. The doctor's comments give an interesting insight into the problems and treatment of mental health during the war. He stated that patients were given the freedom to roam the grounds and were given work to occupy them. Psychotherapy had been tried at the hospital but was discontinued. The fact that this treatment was described as the German system may be a clue as to why this was.

Dr Armstrong-Jones also discussed men from the forces who suffered from shellshock. They were not treated at Claybury as a man could not be classed as insane while he was still in the forces. Claybury did however treat a number of members of the public suffering from shock and fear of Zeppelin raids. According to Dr Armstrong-Jones these were quickly cured. In his opinion there were fewer cases of insanity during the war, owing to there being plenty of work and money.

There was another interesting report concerning Claybury Hospital shortly after when one of the hospital's employees was summonsed for building a fire in the grounds. The fire was reported to have had flames 8ft high and that it was burning during a Zeppelin raid. The man responsible claimed that the fire had been burning for fifteen years. The magistrate dealing with the case said that there seemed to be lunatics outside the asylum who should perhaps be in it.

There seemed to be an unorganised competition in the press to find the Essex family with the most members serving in the forces. Mr and Mrs Samuel Chapman of Norsey Road, Billericay, had six sons in the Army, five serving at the front and one on leave at home after being wounded.

There was an unusual case being heard at East Ham Court in August. It questioned whether a young man who had lived in England all his life but had been born of Hungarian parents was liable for military service. Ernest Green was twenty-two and lived in Capel Road, Forest Gate. He was charged with being an absentee. Green had already been before the local tribunal and argued that he should not have to serve in the British Army when his sympathies were with the country of his parents. He had claimed to be an enemy alien but this was not recognised by the Home Office. The tribunal had found that he could serve the country in a non-combatant role. Green had appealed this decision and still refused to go and join the Army.

The court decided that as he had lived in England all his life and had never seemed to see himself as Hungarian before, he should now join the Army. His father's role was also unclear as he believed himself to be an American citizen after living in the country for some time. This seemed to be another argument against Green's appeal about his father's country, as he had obviously been willing to give up his Hungarian nationality – not something which seemed to show a strong commitment to his nation of birth. The claim of American nationality proved to be false, however, as he had not lived there long enough. The arguments were much too complicated for the court that eventually gave Green leave to appeal against their decision.

There was finally some comfort and some level of revenge for those scared of Zeppelin attacks when on 2 September 1916, Lt William Leefe Robinson from Hornchurch Airfield shot down the *SL11*, which came down at Cuffley. Until this time British aircraft had seemed to have little to offer in the fight against the large airships. Leefe Robinson's guns had been loaded with the new exploding bullets. There had been a cash prize offered for the first Zeppelin brought down over Britain. Although this had earlier been unsuccessfully claimed by gunners at Purfleet their near neighbour from Hornchurch was successful in claiming the prize. This prize had been gathered from British businessmen and amounted to more than £3,000. With the prize money he received for his bravery, Leefe Robinson bought one of the few cars in Hornchurch. The event caused a great deal of interest all over the country and although he was based in Essex, the shooting down of the airship was seen all over London. A description of the event was given by Muriel Dayrell-Browing who watched the airship fall from

Lieutenant William Leefe Robinson became famous overnight for being the first pilot to shoot down an airship over land.

her window. The Zeppelin was caught in the glare of up to twenty searchlights and was being fired on by numerous anti-aircraft guns. The airship then got lost in the clouds and it was only later that it appeared again as a brilliant red light as it fell to the ground on fire.

The lady did not seem to be aware at the time that the airship had been shot down by a British aircraft and thought that it had been hit by anti-aircraft fire. The glare of the burning airship lit up all of London and the cheers were heard from everywhere. She described the death of the crew as the most dramatic deaths in the world's history.

The important role that Hornchurch Airfield (or Suttons Lane to give it its correct name), played in the war became obvious when a few weeks later the Zeppelin *L32* was shot down on 24 September by Frederick Sowery, also from Hornchurch Airfield. The airship came down at Snails Farm, Great Bursted, near Billericay. This was reported in the *Burnham Advertiser* on 30 September 1916. As many of the Zeppelins and aeroplanes that attacked London flew over the Burnham area it was bound to have aroused local interest. The report stated that the destruction of the airship was witnessed by hundreds of people in the area.

This was no surprise as, although some hid under the table for protection during raids, just as many went outside to watch them.

A number of the workers from Kynochtown went and saw the Zeppelin that came down at Billericay. The following comment made by one of them showed how most of the public, or at least women, had no real antagonism against the enemy. They said that the dead crew of the airship only looked about fourteen and that they felt sorry for their mothers back in Germany.

The event had a great effect on some local areas and the road through Romford was full of people on their way to Billericay to see the wreckage. They were on bicycles, motorbikes and more cars than most locals ever thought existed. There was also a sudden fashion in the county for rings made of zinc from the wreckage of the airship.

Respect for the crews of enemy airships or aeroplanes were not always shown. There was a report of German airmen who were shot down over the Dengie Peninsula being buried where they fell, but these men were later dug up and given a proper burial.

Leefe Robinson, Sowery and others officers from Hornchurch were seen on the night of the demise of *L32* in Robinson's car driving away from the airfield at Hornchurch to go and see the wreck.

On same evening another Zeppelin was brought down by a pilot from Essex. The *L33* was shot down by Lt Alfred Bathe Brandon from Hainault Airfield, the same pilot who had been mentioned earlier in relation to the *L15*. The *L33* was not destroyed, however, and landed at Little Wigborough and was set on fire by its crew.

Hornchurch was again the airbase in the news when Lt William Tempest who brought down *L31* on 1 October was also based there. Tempest did manage to set fire to the airship which came down at Potters Bar with no survivors.

In November a lorry carrying wreckage of one of the Zeppelins brought down locally, stopped in Chelmsford High Street. It was besieged by a large crowd of people who took parts of the wreckage as souvenirs. The lorry drove off but when it stopped for petrol it was raided again and had to be protected by soldiers.

After the success of the airmen in bringing down the Zeppelins, raids by the airships began to tail off. Any celebration at this success was very short-lived, as what came instead of the Zeppelins was even worse. They were replaced by aeroplanes and the large German bombers became regular visitors during the following year and led to the first dogfights in the skies above Essex. Shooting down these aircraft was much harder than destroying the airships had been. The raids that were carried out by these aircraft also turned out to be much more lethal than the Zeppelin raids had been.

FOUR

1917

The month of January saw the first battle of Wadi, Iraq, in which the British withdrew from Turkish forces. The Germans announced unrestricted U-boat attacks on allied shipping. The U-boats however, also attacked neutral ships if they thought that they could be carrying war supplies. This was one of the main reasons that America finally entered the war after breaking off diplomatic relations with Germany in February. Also in February, Mata Hari was arrested for spying for the Germans. The case has always raised some questions about the validity of her conviction. She admitted at one point to being a French agent but was accused of being a double agent by a Frenchman George Ladoux who was later arrested as a double agent himself. Mata Hari was executed by firing squad.

The relationship between Germany and America was deteriorating and declined even further after there was an attempt by Germany to get Mexico to declare war on the United States. The plot was discovered and made public.

March saw the overthrow of Czar Nicholas of Russia who then abdicated. April saw the Americans officially declare war on Germany. In the same month much of the French Army mutinied. There were widespread arrests and over 500 men were sentenced to death. Officially only around fifty were executed but it is thought unofficially that the death toll could have been much higher.

There was a successful outcome in one battle when the Canadians took Vimy Ridge. Unfortunately, things did not go as well in other areas. There was another fiasco at the Second Battle of Gaza for which General Archibald Murray was dismissed.

June saw a heavy air raid on London in which 162 died and 432 were injured. This was a clear example of the lethal difference between Zeppelins and aircraft.

July saw the first US troops land in France. The Third Battle of Ypres (Passchendaele) began with the eventual loss of 700,000 men of both sides, many of whom drowned in the mud.

Lawrence of Arabia took Aqaba and Russian troops on the Austrian Front mutinied, for which hundreds were shot. George V changed the name of the royal family to Windsor to distance them from their German origins.

In Loving Memory of
PRIVATE EDWARD WADE.
MACHINE GUN CORPS
WHO WAS WOUNDED 2ND AUGUST
IN THE BATTLE OF YPRES
AND DIED 3RD OCTOBER 1917.
AGED 27 YEARS.
HE NOBLY ANSWERED HIS COUNTRYS CALL
AND GAVE HIS LIFE FOR ONE AND ALL.
GONE FROM US BUT NOT FORGOTTEN.
NEVER SHALL THY MEMORY FADE.
SWEETEST THOUGHTS SHALL EVER LINGER.
AROUND THE SPOT WHERE THOU ART LAID.

The Battle of Ypres may have seemed far away to the residents of Essex but this Essex man was there and he returned home only to end up in Aveley cemetery.

In November the Bolsheviks overthrew the Russian government and Passchendaele was finally taken after three months of fighting. There were further battles at Gaza and Cambrai. December saw the British capture Jerusalem from the Turks.

❖ ❖ ❖

The year began with more restrictions placed on the Essex population. There was to be no more pleasure cruising at night on the Rivers Colne, Blackwater, Crouch, Roach and on the Thames Estuary. Some areas were also restricted during the day but a licence could be obtained from the police for some use of the rivers for pleasure.

Mersea Island, along with other Essex islands, was closely guarded against waterborne invasion attempts.

While the sailors could not use the river however, they were offered the chance of other, drier pleasures. An advertisement for the Electric Theatre in Mersea Road, Colchester, stated that it was not only a privilege but also a duty to see the film of the Battle of Ancre and the advance of the tanks.

Some of the restrictions that had been imposed on the population did not go down well with everyone. A letter to *The Times* on 13 January from R.B. Tollington from Tendring Rectory, Weeley, complained that he had been refused a licence to read German newspapers. It seems that he had been doing so for years and thought that it was a good way to understand the enemy.

There had been problems throughout the war in convincing married men that they should go and fight while single men were still at home. Conscription changed the situation to some degree but there were still some discontent over married men with large families being called up while many young single men still escaped service due to working in munitions. It was not just the men themselves who were grumbling about this situation but local Boards of Guardians. If a married man went away to fight then there was a good chance that the board may have to support his family. This obviously was not the case with single men.

The Romford tribunal began the year by hearing the case of a young man of nineteen whose mother said that she needed him at home to look after her. She had already lost one son to the war and had two more already serving. The tribunal decided that she would be as well off financially with her son in the forces and although she may have needed looking after it was too bad as everyone had to do their bit. This shows the variations in tribunal decisions as another tribunal in Billericay had earlier excused a baker who had to look after his mother.

Another soap that was very useful for the men in the trenches.

The Green, Harlow.

Harlow before the war was very different to how it looked after the new town was built much later.

Being in business did not influence the Romford tribunal. They also heard the plea of a businessman to be excused service as he had put all his money into his business and would lose it if he had to enlist. They decided that there had been enough time for him to find someone else to run the business.

Epping tribunal found that a steam plough mechanic should not be exempt from service, which seems a strange decision in relation to the need for food production. They decided to defer his service by two months however, so a replacement could be found. This seems to have been a common decision. Deferment was preferable to outright decisions to excuse men from service.

Many of the people at home felt that they were suffering due to the war. Food stocks were becoming short and it seemed that even the weather was going against those struggling along at home. The winter was one of the worst for some time as the frosts lasted well into April. The hardships suffered by those at home did not however seem so bad compared to soldiers returning home on leave from the front. There was often a great deal of misunderstanding between what was happening at the front and the public perception of it. Many men were happy to get back to their units where everyone understood what they were going through, despite the return to atrocious conditions.

The refusal of the tribunals to excuse many of the working men that came before them from military service seems to show a class bias in their decision-making. There did seem to be more of a choice for those of the officer class. When Edward Craggs, a former officer in the Sportsman's Battalion, was in court in Chelmsford applying for a discharge of his bankruptcy there was no mention of sending him to serve in the forces. He had resigned his commission in the Sportsman's Battalion due to his financial problems and was, it seems, allowed to stay at home if that was what he wished to do. Private soldiers did not have the chance of resigning from their service regardless whatever their problems were.

In a reversal of the last situation a man managed to escape criminal charges by going to fight. It was not only British criminals that Essex had to deal with. Lewis Mened was a private in the Canadian Construction Unit and was charged with stealing four cockerels from Aveley Hall Farm. One of his officers stood up for him in court and said that until then his record had been unblemished. He also stated that the unit would soon be going overseas. The prosecutor then said that if the defendant wanted to go and do his duty they would not proceed with the charges.

The courts were kept busy with a number of cases and in some events it seemed that everyone was stealing from each other. William Simpson, a soldier, pleaded guilty to stealing half a pound of cake and half a pound of currants from a house in Frinton-on-Sea. One of his officers was in court and said that the Army didn't want him back. There had been no reason for him to steal food, as there was plenty available to him. They suspected that he did it to try to get out of the Army. He achieved this goal for three months at least while he was in prison serving his sentence.

While soldiers were stealing from the public, the public were also stealing from soldiers. Mary Smith and Alice Bunton, both nineteen, were factory hands at

Waltham Abbey with horses and carts waiting outside about the time of the First World War.

Chelmsford and were charged with stealing sausages at a military ball, property of the Secretary of State for War. Their argument was that a soldier had told them that they could have what they wanted. They were described as bad girls who were seriously in need of some correction. Bunton was given borstal training. Smith was obviously not as bad a girl as her friend and so was not sent to borstal but to a Salvation Army home for two years.

The wreckage of one of the Zeppelins downed in Essex was put to a good use. There was a sale of the remnants of *L33* at the Moot Hall, Colchester, in aid of the Red Cross. Music was supplied by military bands and there was also a display of German implements of war, including caps, helmets and even bombs,

PROMENADE GARDENS. CLACTON-ON-SEA

Well-kept gardens on the seafront were always a popular attraction such as this one at Clacton.

by Bernard Afford of Witham. Small pieces of the aluminium from one of the Zeppelins were sold and raised £40. The mayor and other dignitaries were the stallholders.

Women had by this time began to take much more structured roles in war work when several new female units were formed. These included the Women's Army Auxiliary Corps. The female recruits replaced male soldiers as cooks, tailors, bakers and orderlies, etc. This then released the men who had been doing these jobs to fight. The women lived in camps or barracks in the same way as the men did.

A woman going out to work was not as straightforward as it seemed and was causing some problems according to a report from a doctor in the *Essex Times*. This was because hospitals were so full of wounded soldiers that civilian patients often had to be released earlier which extended the convalescent period to be spent at home. This was far from ideal as there often was little chance of the patient being fed the correct diet that they needed as there was an appalling lack of cooking facilities in most homes. The fact that many mothers and wives were also not at home but at work also hindered this.

This did little to help get important workers back to fitness and back to work. The report went on to say how many of the invalids were being looked after by the older children of the family while the mother went to work. One carer, when told to give a sick child a poached egg, said the child looked bemused. The child apparently said, 'Can't we just go and buy an egg instead?' She thought that a poached egg was a stolen one.

Some of the public houses in Chelmsford dated back some time and the King's Head must have been popular with local troops.

As well as the Women's Auxiliary Army Corps there was also a Women's Royal Naval Service started in which women did the same jobs as their counterparts in the Army; replacing men but only on shore – not at sea. The Women's Royal Air Force did the same kinds of jobs. There was also a women's Land Army formed to help out in agriculture.

A meeting was called at the Chelmsford Empire in February to discuss the king's appeal for volunteers for the new Army of home defence. There was already a Chelmsford company of the Essex Volunteer Regiment that numbered 150. There was a feeling at the meeting that there should have been more men in the company in a town the size of Chelmsford. Many smaller towns in the county had similar-sized companies but from a much lower population.

In February a National Service Scheme came into operation for those aged between eighteen and sixty and not in military service. This was to assist in industry. It meant that workers could be directed to take up essential war work even if they had to move away to another district to do so.

Not everyone was happy with this situation and there was a tribunal set up to deal with workers' difficulties, similar to the tribunals for those who were trying to get out of military service. A cabinet-maker/carpenter from Cleethorpes went before the Colchester tribunal and claimed that he could not live on his wages as he had to keep two homes going, one in Cleethorpes and one in Essex. His job was making aircraft propellers and as important war work he needed a certificate if he wanted to leave his employer.

The Essex Times *printed an article stating that one reason some believed for the safety of the cathedral in Chelmsford during an air raid was the prayers of those inside.*

HAMILTON AVE. N.Z. CONVALESCENT CAMP HORNCHURCH.

The convalescent camp for New Zealand soldiers at Hornchurch.

It was found that the man was not a munitions volunteer who been transferred to the area but had got the job from the labour exchange. Volunteers directed to other areas were entitled to an extra allowance but he was not. His employer argued that he could not be replaced and he was refused a leaving certificate.

A report from Romford Workhouse in February gave the number of inmates as 423. There were also 71 wounded soldiers in the military block. The sister in charge, Miss Gibson, said that the soldiers were given numerous gifts and entertainment for which they were very grateful. It seems that despite being in the workhouse, wounded soldiers did have slightly better treatment than the normal workhouse inmate.

There were still attempts by some groups to maintain some level of normality in their lives despite the war. There was a meeting at the Horn Hotel in Braintree by the East Essex Hounds. They decided to carry on hunting the following season under the master Mr R. Duke Hill. It would seem that not all the horses had been taken by the Army.

There had been a Royal Warrant on military pensions passed in February. Some of the clauses stated that not all medically unfit members of the forces who had originally been passed fit to serve, nor all widows and dependants of soldiers who had died during service or while pensioners, would get pensions. There were no full pensions for unmarried or separated wives. This was to be a point that raised a lot of questions during the conflict as the morals of society seemed to be under pressure, especially in regard to children born out of wedlock.

The shortages of food began to have an effect on people by this time and at Southend a fruit and vegetable salesman was charged with selling potatoes at a

BEACH & PALACE HOTEL, SOUTHEND.

The size of the Palace Hotel showed how popular Southend had become as a seaside resort.

higher than permitted price. He had sold them at 12s a hundredweight to several people and was fined £12.

The first two years of the war had led to few food shortages but this was to change by 1917. The shortage began with potatoes and for a time it was impossible to get any. Although bread was never rationed, the price did go up to 1s a loaf in early 1917. This led to the government subsidising the cost by paying 3d towards the cost of each loaf sold, a tremendous expense for the country and an enlightened move for the time. Rationing of some items was to come later.

There were numerous small relief agencies started around the county to help those involved in the war. At Colchester, the North Station Comforts Fund made

Soldiers often had their photos taken in uniform to send to their families. This man was someone's Uncle Fred.

sure that wounded soldiers were given tea and refreshments when arriving or leaving from the town.

There was an interesting story concerning the West Ham tribunal in the *Essex Times* in March. A Mr T.W. Stout claimed that he had taken life vows to devote himself to spiritual work at the Essex Leper Colony at East Hadingfield (I have also found this as being located at Bicknacre). It was the only leper colony in the country and had four lepers living there. The members of the tribunal felt that a strong young man like Stout should be in the Army as his work could be done by someone else. Then one of the tribunal asked if any members of the board would do the job for £100. It seemed that they would not as the case was then referred to the county tribunal.

The idea of there being lepers in the country during the war seems a strange one when one sees the disease as something that people suffered from in the Middle Ages or in Asia. In fact before 1914 and the foundation of the St Giles Home for British Lepers, there had been no provision for lepers in the country. Many of the patients had in fact contracted the disease while serving in outposts of the Empire. As it was not a notifiable disease, there were no accurate figures for sufferers but it was thought that there were as many as between forty and fifty sufferers in the country with only one of those who had caught the disease in England.

The St Giles Home was described as looking like a cottage hospital in an article in *The Times* in October 1921. It seems that the home was little known before *The Times* published the article. As with the man who tried to be excused service in the forces due to his work at St Giles, the staff were described as giving their lives to the home.

The cases varied in age and background with elderly men and children as young as fifteen being infected with the disease. One child, a boy, died after six months at the home and he was the only case of someone in England catching the disease. He had never left the country but had a brother who had also died of the disease while abroad. Many of the men in the home had their wives living with them.

There were numerous examples of fundraising for good causes around the county. In Romford in April there was an auction in aid of St Dunstan's Clinic for blind servicemen. It was held at the Corn Exchange and organised by the Voluntary Aid Detachment, Essex 51. They had help from the special constables and wounded soldiers who did much of the work.

The first lot sold was a table centre made by a wounded soldier at Romford Military Hospital. It sold for 10s. Many of the lots were bought and then given back to be sold once again, boosting the amount raised. This included a Burmese sword, which sold for £2 and was then resold for £1 17s 6d. Private Gates of the Artist Rifles, who were by this time based in Romford, was the auctioneer for part of the proceedings and £115 was raised.

Another fundraising event in Romford was a football match, Essex versus the Army at the Great Eastern Railway sports ground at Romford. A crowd of around 1,000, mainly soldiers, watched the match. The proceeds were in aid of Great Eastern Railway employees serving in the forces who were being held prisoner in Germany. The Artist Rifles band played before the match and at half time.

Raphael Park in Romford was named after Sir Herbert Raphael who gave the land to the local council. No doubt he and his comrades used the park when they were based at Hare Hall Camp.

Although the commonly held view is that everyone in the country was most patriotic and were doing their best for the war effort, this was not always the case. *The Times* reported in May on a dock strike at Tilbury by men who had been promised 1s 6d a day war bonus but who were only paid 1s a day bonus. As food shortages were beginning to bite all over the country by this time, a strike by dockworkers seems to have been quite unpatriotic.

While British workers were going on strike, other workers were found to boost the workforce. There was a development in the use of German prisoners of war as workers in May when the first of them to be used as farm workers in the county arrived at Fox Burrow Farm in Barkingside. There were seventy-five of them and they were to live in the farm buildings and have thirty-five guards. They went out in small groups, usually of five, to work. The men seemed pleased to be relieved of the normal monotony of captivity and to get out of the camps.

The Billericay Board of Guardians received a letter from the Local Government Board concerning the Royal Warrant issued in February in relation to the relief of disabled men discharged from the Army. It stated that any pensioned men who were disabled due to the war and needed special treatment but were unable to care for themselves or their family, would get an allowance in lieu of their pension.

This would be not less than 27s 6d a week with a deduction for maintenance. If the man had to be away from home for treatment, his wife would get an amount equivalent to a widow's pension plus an allowance for any children. Although these rules were set they were not always carried out to the letter as will be seen later.

The welfare of workers at home during the war was not forgotten and the Sterling Telephone and Electrical Company in Dagenham had opened an athletic

The old mill was still standing in Barking although it did not seem to have any sails by the First World War, so could not have still been in use.

The rural and sparsely populated road between Barking and Dagenham which was to become lined with council houses when Becontree estate was built after the war.

club for their staff on 5 acres of ground adjoining their works. The club was opened by John Bethell MP, who said in his speech that he could see no reason why the women employed at the factory, who were now in the majority, could not form football teams. As mentioned earlier, Kynoch and Company already had women's teams. As it turned out the Sterling club formed a women's team and it became a very good one.

An interesting point was also made about the workforce at Sterlings in an article. Although the factory was based in Dagenham, the workforce were listed as coming mainly from Barking, East Ham, Romford and Ilford. Dagenham at this time was of course no more than a small village whose population would have been too low to provide the large workforce Sterlings needed. A change was to come later when Dagenham became more of an industrial centre than the other areas with a larger workforce, after the Greater London Council built the Becontree council estate between the wars.

A large Dagenham house, Valence. Although rural, Dagenham was to become the site of the largest council housing estate in the world shortly after the war.

Dagenham was still a very rural place during the war. Although it had large factories such as Sterlings, it was essentially a small village with some large houses in the area such as Fanshawe's, seen here.

The defence of Harwich had been reliant on Landguard Fort in Felixstowe for some time, although new guns were added to Beacon Hill on the Essex side of the harbour.

The defences for Harwich Harbour were mainly based on the Suffolk side of the bay at Felixstowe. This included a seaplane base.

Harwich was the victim of a large air attack in July when between twelve and fourteen enemy planes attacked the town. Eleven people were killed and thirty-six were injured. The continuation of air raids had led to calls for revenge raids on Germany in many national newspapers. This did not go down well with some people. The Bishop of Chelmsford was disgusted with the calls for reprisal air raids. He pointed out that the same newspapers had been very vocal in condemning the savagery of air raids on women and children by Germans and now they called for the same to be done by British airmen to women and children in Germany. Other churchmen agreed with the bishop and the Revd Mr Hudson from the parish church at East Ham wondered how Christians could consider that air raids were acceptable to those with their religious belief. Hudson's colleague, the Revd C.E. Thomas, also from East Ham, had a different view. He said that reprisals were, from a Christian point of view, acceptable. He obviously believed in an eye for an eye.

The upkeep of local cottage hospitals was reported on in the local press. In July the *Essex Times* stated that the Victoria Cottage Hospital in Romford had six admissions in the past month while two patients were discharged. There were twelve patients: seven adults and five children. Four operations had been carried out that week. Gifts were given of milk by Mrs Billey, eggs by Mr Abrahams, flowers by Mr Lapwood, fruit and books from an anonymous source, more fruit by Mrs Moore and Lady Turner gave men's shirts and linen.

Despite the war, crime was still evident and a young soldier found himself removed from one institution, the Army, to go to another, Borstal. Eighteen-year-old Frederick Scarbrow was found guilty at Barking of breaking into the home of Samuel Fields.

Another crime, this time without a victim, was committed by Jane Bushell of Stamford Rivers who was in court charged with attempted suicide. She was found in a pond but was rescued and taken to Ongar Workhouse. She gave the reason for her attempt as domestic troubles.

The summer brought the revival of sports among those able to spare the time for them. Most of those young enough to take part were in service so it was mainly the Army units that pursued sporting pastimes. At Thorpe le Soken the Army Service Corps had a sports day and after a cricket match they held a concert.

The Barking Disablement Sub Committee had eleven meetings throughout the year and surprisingly only had nineteen applications for supplementary pensions. Of these only eight were confirmed while two were given temporary payments. Seven were already earning too much and so did not qualify. One was refused as his level of pre-enlistment dependency differed from the findings of the pension office. This again seems to be a case of someone being passed fit for service who should not have been. Since 1 July 1916 the committee had been notified of 187 men who had been invalided out of the Army and of these 114 had got a job. It seems that those who were made invalids during the war were much more likely to find work while the conflict still went on due to high demand for war goods. This situation was to change dramatically for invalids after the war.

The bathing machines on Dovercourt beach show what a popular seaside resort it had become.

It wasn't only the men of Barking who were facing danger from the war. Although many industries of the time were not as safe for the workers as they could have been, things were to get worse during the war. There had already been a major disaster at a TNT factory in Silvertown in January when not only was the local area devastated but there were 73 deaths and 400 injuries after the factory exploded.

Another factory that had turned to war work was the Ajax Chemical works in Barking, which had entered into the production of shells. In August there was an explosion at the factory following a fire and 13 died.

The report in *The Times* stated that the building was of brick and was two storeys high. It was 60ft wide and 100ft long. The number of casualties turned out to be low as there would normally have been around 150 women and girls in the building. Luckily the explosion occurred just as the shifts were changing and few workers were present. There were quite detailed reports in *The Times* of the incident which was unusual as the earlier disaster at Silvertown was less well reported despite being much more serious. There were later claims that the Silvertown incident had been hushed up because of the adverse effect on public morale.

The report on the Ajax explosion in the local newspaper, the *Barking, Ilford and East Ham Advertiser*, gave a list of the names of all the victims. It also mentioned how the factory was one of a number that had recently been located in Hertford Road near the border with East Ham.

Aircraft had by this time replaced the use of Zeppelins in air raids and seemed to be much more lethal in their use. In August, Southend was once again the victim of an air raid but unlike the early Zeppelin raids that led to few deaths, this one was much more serious. A dozen planes attacked the town, which was full of holidaymakers at the time. There were 23 people killed in various parts of the town.

In Leigh-on-Sea, a horse and a dog were also killed in the raid when Cliffsea Grove was hit; three houses were destroyed and three more damaged. A special constable named Heap was passing on his bicycle calling up other specials and was 40ft away from an exploding bomb. It knocked him off his bicycle but he was not seriously hurt.

Walton on the Naze was still a quiet backwater by the time the war broke out. Its popularity as a seaside resort came later.

Air raid warnings in the town were updated after this raid when the Mayor, Alderman Joseph Francis, stated that there would be warning sirens fitted to the electricity and gas works.

The raid at Southend was witnessed by a lady from Brentwood and her account was printed in the *Essex Times*. Mrs Pond was the wife of Gunner Pond who lived in Hart Street, Brentwood. She had been staying at Southend but went home before the raid took place but then went back for the day with her two-year-old daughter on Sunday 12 August. After a pleasant day by the sea she returned to the Great Eastern Railway station in time to catch the 6.15 p.m. train back to Brentwood. There were some aircraft circling overhead but everyone seemed to believe that they were British planes as there was no panic among the crowds. Mrs Pond got on the train and before it left a bomb fell close to the station. Those on the train got off and ran to a waiting room carrying Mrs Pond and her daughter with them in the crush. A bomb fell by the window and killed seven of the people in the room, injuring many others. A soldier and a sailor who were in the crowd were trying to get everyone out of the room and telling them to lay down, which was the safest thing to do. They were forcing some people down onto the ground who tried to run away in panic. Mrs Pond counted nine more bombs; most of them were almost on top of the crowds in the station. When the raid was over, a new guard had to be found for the train as the original man had been killed. Many of the passengers arriving at the station were by this time bandaged as they were suffering from minor wounds. They told how they had to step over bodies lying in the street to get to the station. The story shows how a simple day out at the seaside ended in tragedy during the war.

The Chelmsford tribunal that decided whether men could be excused military service had been criticised in *The Times*. It seems that in April the tribunal had excused a number of men under the age of thirty from service. Members of the tribunal argued that this had occurred before Sir William Robertson's call for a further 500,000 men and that the decision to excuse these men would now be reviewed. Local decisions did not always seem reliable compared to those in other areas.

The market at Romford was still selling livestock during the war.

By 1917, food shortages had become more common and in many places, such as Colchester, allotments were given out to the population so that they could grow their own food. Potatoes were one of the more popular things to grow as they had become so scarce. At one point the mayor of the town commandeered large quantities of margarine, which was also in short supply. It was then sold at a regular price at certain outlets. It was not only food that was scarce; matches were also in short supply, which was a real hardship at the time. Queues began to appear outside shops and the police would often disperse anyone queuing before 7.30 a.m. Some families had the idea to send their children out to save a place in the queue from as early as 5.00 a.m. which was an obvious reason for the police action.

In an attempt to rectify the food problems, the government set maximum prices for many items of food. This was not a popular move with farmers. Oscar Grey of Bretts Hall, Tendring, put the farmer's view in a letter to *The Times*. He stated how much land went out of production due to low prices as it was impossible for farmers to grow food at a loss. The low food prices were to the benefit of the industrial classes whose wages had risen because of the increase in war work, but ruined farmers. The government had already taken the wool crop and restricted the sale of hay, which meant that farmers had received below market prices for both items. Even the 'grow for victory' campaign among the public was proving difficult for farmers as the increased demand for seed potatoes to grow on allotments meant higher prices for seed for farmers as well, who then

Boy Scout groups had been formed in most areas by the time of the war and played a part in protecting the Home Front. Commissioner Noble had formed the Seven Kings group in 1909.

had to sell what they grew from the high-priced seed at the low prices set by the government. Mr Grey would seem to have had a point.

Rationing, when it finally came, was a relief to many, although organising the system was not easy. The schools in Colchester were closed for a week as the teachers were employed in filling out ration cards for the population, which were then distributed by Boy Scouts.

The first item rationed was sugar in the autumn when ration cards for the commodity were given out. Special supplies were given to those who grew fruit for preservation. It was to be the following year, however, that rationing of other items took hold.

One Essex man seemed to have made a lot of money out of the food situation in the country. Arthur Heading was a potato salesman who had lived in Goodmayes in his own house which he had paid £420 for. Then he moved to Cambridgeshire into a house that cost £1,000. He then bought a farm for £5,500. It seems his good fortune and progress was not entirely legal. Mr Heading was remanded on sixteen summonses under the Seed Potato Order as he had made £224 more than

Witham was already quite a large town by the time of the First World War. As with other towns it had its own troops billeted there.

he was allowed to by selling them, even if he had been charging the maximum of £12 per ton. He was fined £320 and sent to prison for six weeks.

The lack of food and the resulting decline in health was supposedly one reason why illness was so bad later in the year but by September the report of the Romford Medical Officer of Health did not seem too bad. There was one case of scarlet fever in Rainham, one of enteric fever and diphtheria in Hornchurch, one case of TB in Hornchurch and one in Chadwell Heath along with seven cases of measles in Havering. There had also been twelve deaths.

There were still problems with finding soldiers billets in the county and not everyone did their best to help. Arthur Collins, a railway signalman from West Hornden, was at Brentwood Petty Sessions in September charged with refusing to billet soldiers in his home. Collins had a three-bedroom house with only three people living in it. He was told that two soldiers would be billeted with him for two nights. Collins argued that his union had told him that members were not to allow soldiers to be billeted in their homes. Another example of patriotism? He was told by the billeting officer that the Army Act overrode union rules. Collins replied that he would chuck the soldiers out if they came. When they did arrive, Privates Cook and Seymour of the 5th Labour Battalion found the house empty and after a long wait had to be billeted elsewhere. Collins was fined 40s.

In October the flu epidemic was beginning to cause serious problems in the county. Many of the schools that had stayed open were now closed. There were thought to be more than 100,000 deaths from flu in Essex alone. The treatment of illness and injuries was still rather archaic in many areas and it was only in

This was one German airship that never made it home. This photograph was supposedly taken in the Thames Estuary.

1917 that the council at Barking decided to try to raise the money for a motor ambulance. The thought of how slowly those involved in accidents must have been taken to hospital before is frightening.

Accidents did not only occur in Barking. In Hornchurch there was a tragic accident that resulted in the death of Private H. Mitchell. What made the accident even more tragic was that Mitchell was a member of the New Zealand Expeditionary Force and had come from New Zealand, fought in Gallipoli and then been killed in a motor accident in Hornchurch. When one considers the rarity of cars on the road, this form of death must have been very unlucky.

Mitchell had been about to go on leave and had been out for the evening in Hornchurch with a friend and both were under the influence of alcohol. There were questions asked about why the two men were out of the hospital at the time as both were wounded and in hospital blues. The driver of the car involved was Alfred Snell, a mechanic in the Royal Flying Corps, who had been driving one of the squadron cars from Sutton's Lane Airfield to Hornchurch when he saw the two men in the road in his headlights. He sounded the horn but as he got close to the men one of them seemed to push the other in front of the car, as a result Mitchell was impaled on the front starting handle. Although Mitchell survived the initial collision, he died a few days later. As the other man had been moved to another hospital and was not in court to give evidence, the case was adjourned.

Braintree was another large town in the county by the outbreak of war. It was obviously a busy day when this photograph was taken.

The number of wounded inevitably grew as the war went on. This group at Chelmsford show their status by wearing blue uniforms.

The flu epidemic did not just strike at home. It had been rife in the trenches in France for some time. John Chessire, a member of the Sportsman's Battalion, suffered from the illness and described how bad it was and how it had such an effect on the head. He also said that the Germans had been hit even worse by the disease and wondered if this was one of the reasons that the last big push by the Germans in an attempt to win the war before the Americans arrived had broken down.

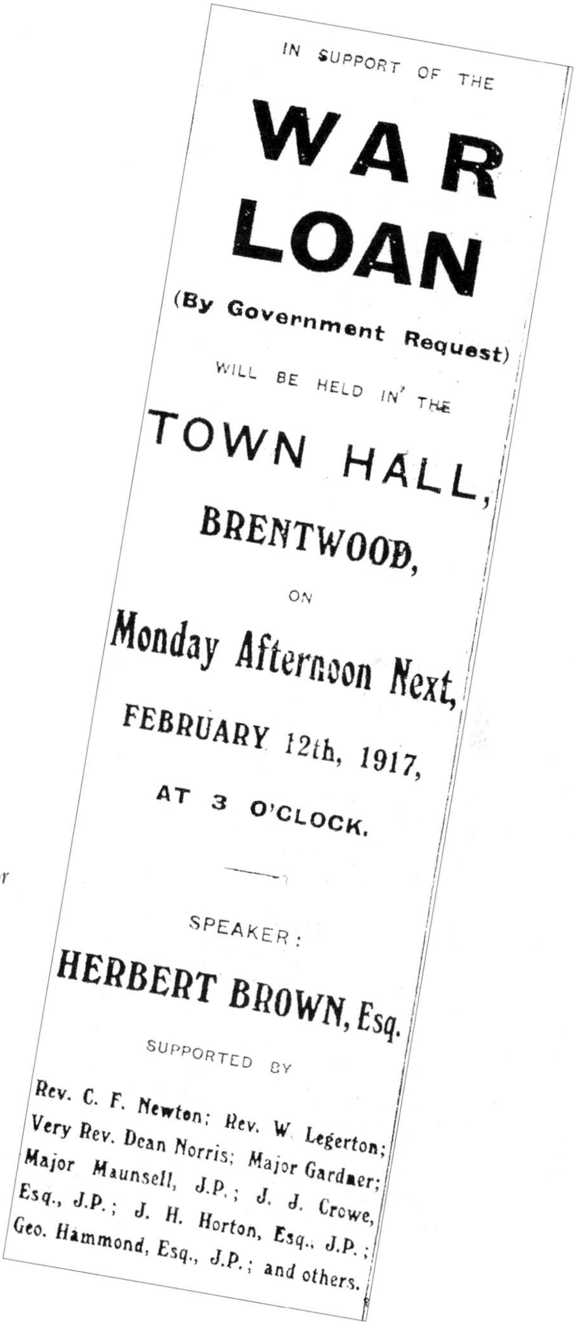

IN SUPPORT OF THE

WAR LOAN

(By Government Request)

WILL BE HELD IN' THE

TOWN HALL, BRENTWOOD,

ON

Monday Afternoon Next, FEBRUARY 12th, 1917, AT 3 O'CLOCK.

SPEAKER:

HERBERT BROWN, Esq.

SUPPORTED BY

Rev. C. F. Newton; Rev. W. Legerton; Very Rev. Dean Norris; Major Gardner; Major Maunsell, J.P.; J. J. Crowe, Esq., J.P.; J. H. Horton, Esq., J.P.; Geo. Hammond, Esq., J.P.; and others.

Requests for money to pay for the war were quite common in most towns. This one was advertised in the local newspaper in 1917.

Even rationing became a subject for postcards during the war. This queue was for potatoes that were very scarce at one point.

Despite the constant reports of the German mistreatment of British POWs, a letter in the *Essex Times* from a Romford man being held in Germany gave another side to the story. Although the letter stated that officers were treated better than privates in captivity, he described the camp he was in at Brunswick. They had books, a theatre with props and even a cinema. One of the prisoners was even allowed to keep a pet dog; none of which sounds like particularly harsh treatment.

There are several reports of how wages were much higher during the war and that poverty had decreased, but the poor condition that children lived in had not always been changed by higher wages. At East Ham Court in December Charles Glover, a munitions worker from Woolwich Arsenal, and his wife Alice were charged with the neglect of their nine children. The case was brought by the NSPCC. Despite Glover earning over £4 a week and the family receiving another 12s from their eldest daughter who also worked, there were serious complaints as to how Mrs Glover was keeping the home. A school attendance officer had called at the house and noticed how dirty the children were. Some of them were suffering from scabies. Despite being well fed they were filthy and their bedding was described as foul smelling. The only furniture in the house was in the kitchen and one bed had a wooden door as a mattress. There seemed to have been no washing done for some time and the court wondered what they did with their money. It was of course the mother who was blamed, as the court put no blame on the husband as he was working to help the war effort. They considered sending Mrs Glover to prison but worried about what would happen to the children. They decided that the children would be better off in the workhouse and sentenced Mrs Glover to six weeks' hard labour.

Brigadier General Ovens made a speech to the Thanet Volunteers at the end of the year and said that there was still a danger of invasion. Because of this, he said, every man should join the volunteers. The brigadier was scathing in his criticism of the Romford volunteers who he said had numbered 200 at the beginning of the war when commanded by Mr Lewis. This was when the men had to pay for their own uniforms, firing practice and transport. Now that the War Office paid for this the numbers in the Romford group had dwindled and only around twenty of the original members still remained.

FIVE

1918

The year began with turmoil among some of the smaller states of Europe that were once part of Russia. One of these situations was caused when the Cossacks declared their own state independent. The founding of the Republic of Don led to the Russian Civil War. In February Trotsky ended the war with the Germans and in March gave up large parts of the old Russian Empire, including Poland. Also in March the Russians and the Germans signed a treaty.

Released from the war on the Eastern Front the Germans launched a major offensive on the Western Front in March in an attempt to end the war before the Americans arrived in force. The allies gave up more land than had been won in the previous four years of the war; in one case the Germans advanced 40 miles in a week. A notice appeared in *The Times* written by Rudyard Kipling stating that 'We are fighting for our lives.'

In April the Royal Flying Corps and the Royal Naval Air Service amalgamated to become the Royal Air Force.

The German success continued until July by which time more Americans had arrived at the front. The Spanish Flu epidemic had also begun to hit the men at the front and some thought that this may have played a part in the decline in German fortunes as by July the German advance seemed to have run out of steam.

August saw the beginning of the Battle of Amiens when Canadian and Australian troops began to push the Germans back again. There seemed to be endless victories for the Allies reversing the failure of the previous months. The Allied offensive that began in August four years after the war had begun was successful in pushing Germans back even further.

In October Hungary split from Austria and both countries gave up their part in the war along with Turkey. The U-boat war was suspended and at one point the German Navy mutinied.

The war ended in November and although the Allied forces marched to the borders of Germany, they did not cross into what was to become occupied territory until December.

A German U-boat that was no longer capable of sinking allied ships. It was being towed along the Thames after being captured.

Although the Defence of the Realm regulations had been in operation for some time, they were still used to forbid the taking of photos, sketching or making plans in a large number of areas around the country. Many of these areas were in Essex.

The treatment of wounded and sick ex-servicemen was still a problem in many areas of the county. In Barking there were sixty-three applications for war pensions, which were agreed. The pension committee also stated that arrangements for discharged servicemen who had spent time in sanatoriums were wholly inadequate. They called for the power to put ex-servicemen suffering from tuberculosis in separated cottages in the countryside with fresh healthy air. A similar idea to this was also put forward by others looking at the problem and there were plans to place convalescing officers on farms so that they would learn about agriculture.

The Romford School managers meeting decided that it would be desirable to open a nursery in the town for the care of children whose mothers were working. This would prevent the practice of keeping older children off school to look after their younger brothers and sisters. The opening of a nursery would fill a need that also existed in many other towns.

The unplanned results of war were to be seen in many areas as there were 1,150 centres for the care of mothers and children in the country but there was a need for 5,000 more. One must wonder if these centres would have existed if there had not been a need for women workers in munitions factories. A fund for child

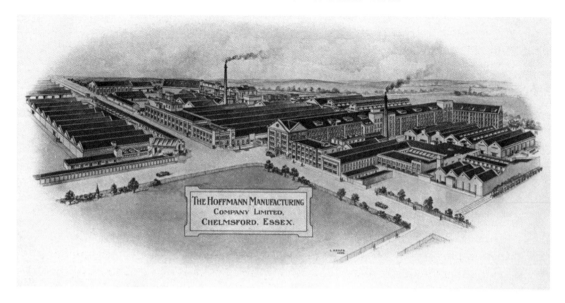

Hoffmanns was one of the factories in Chelmsford which was busy during the First World War.

Ploughing with a team of horses was a skilful job and experience in this work was one reason that men could be excused service in the forces.

welfare was being started and there was to be a jewel appeal, which it was hoped, would be supported by all women giving a good piece of jewellery. This would obviously have been aimed at the middle classes and above.

Although there had not been a shortage of meat until this time, there was a sudden and seemingly unexplained scarcity leading to rationing of all meat, in the south of the country first, then rolled out nationwide. Margarine was also rationed at the same time. Later in the year jam and tea were added to the rationed items list.

The food shortages led to a crackdown on anything that was not within the regulations relating to food. Charles Bartropp, a baker from Margaretting, was fined 10s for not having proper weights at his place of business. An advertisement in the *Essex County Standard* gave a novel way of saving scarce tea. It advised its readers to drink coffee instead at breakfast time.

Brentwood Food Control Committee met with tradesmen to discuss the situation relating to butter and margarine. The tradesmen argued that supplies must be shared equally to avoid starvation. They complained that some of the Food Control Committee was hard on retailers. It was decided that supplies would be distributed to retailers on the basis of the number of customers registered with each one. This would have seemed the reasonable method of doing it from the outset.

There was another hearing into the death of Private Henry Mitchell of the New Zealand forces who had died after a road accident in Hornchurch in 1917. This time the man's friend who had been with him on the evening of the accident, Private John Sterling was in court. He told the court that he had not pushed his friend into the path of the car but had been trying to pull him clear.

The donkey pulling the small cart seems resigned to waiting outside the Prince of Wales in Ingatestone.

Major Cuthbert Round of the Royal Flying Corps had also been in the car and supported the driver's view of events. A verdict of accidental death was given.

There was also a final outcome in another court case from the previous year. George Henry Rainbow and his wife Ellen Elizabeth of Hardwicke Street, Barking, were in court to hear the decision on the death of their daughter who had been one of the girls who had died in the explosion at the Ajax shell works in Barking, the previous year. Under the Working Men's Compensation Act, Mr and Mrs Rainbow were awarded £100 and £8 3s costs in full settlement of the death of their daughter.

It was not only German bombs that were causing damage to Essex homes; in February Easton Lodge in Dunmow caught fire. It was the home of the Earl and Countess of Warwick. The earl was an invalid and had to be rescued by his servants. The countess managed to save some valuables from a safe before escaping. The main part of the house was saved from total destruction.

There was a bold move in relation to air raids in Romford early in the year. Until this time air raid sirens had only been sounded before midnight. From early 1918 on they would be sounded at anytime of the day or night to warn of a raid.

The harsh winter was causing severe problems to the county due to heavy snowfall. The River Roding had overflowed and flooded much of the south of the county. In Ilford, allotments and the golf club were flooded and in Lea Bridge Road trams and trolley buses were travelling through water up to their axles. The north of the county was also affected with the area around Bishop's Stortford looking like the sea.

The loss of men at the front was causing grief among those at home, in some cases it was too much to bear. Joseph Jowers, aged sixty-three, a labourer of Park Gate Farm in Little Clacton had lost one son to the war and another had been badly wounded. As a result he hanged himself in a shed.

Not all soldiers were at the front at this time and Private Wilfred Elmore, aged thirty-four, was charged with causing grievous bodily harm to PC Henry Jones at Leyton. PC Jones had seen a woman come out of a house with an injured face followed by Elmore who had blood on his clothes. When approached, Elmore attacked the PC. Elmore had two previous convictions for violence and was sentenced to ten months' hard labour.

In Romford there was a Food Economy Campaign when Sir Arthur Yapp, the Director of Food Economy, said that the population of Britain was facing its greatest crisis in history. They should therefore dispense with luxury and extravagance.

Although there seems to have been a belief that sex was a subject that only raised its head between married couples during the war, this would seem to have been far from the truth. According to Spike Mays in Reuben's Corner in rural Essex, sex between very young single people was very common. Even children as young as twelve were often sexually active. W.S. Ferrie, a member of the Sportsman's Battalion based in Romford, had also described local girls as making themselves cheap.

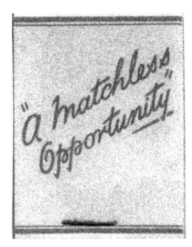

A fundraising matchbook for Brentwood Hospital.

Even the matches inside were marked with the hospital's name.

There are other cases that seem to bear out this lack of morals during the war. Mary Smith of Brentwood Road, Hornchurch, was arrested on a charge of the murder of a young male child whose body was found in a well in the garden of her home. The suspicion was that the baby had been hers and it was claimed in court that she had led a fast life, going out with a number of different men. It was also claimed that she had admitted to a former servant that she had been pregnant. Despite this, after being examined by two doctors and spending months on remand in Holloway Prison, she was found not to have had a baby and was eventually found not guilty of the crime.

Close to the scene of the dead baby in the well, a well-known author of the time, Charles Perfect, found a package while walking one morning on the Mill Park allotments in Hornchurch. The package turned out to be the body of a baby. The suspicion was that the baby had been stillborn but its strange disposal would seem to point to suspicious circumstances as to its birth.

The children obviously found the sight of a photographer very interesting outside the Queen Victoria pub in Theydon Bois.

There was also an inquest on a young lady at Purfleet Military Hospital. Kate Swallow of Heybridge had been in service at the Old Rectory at Orsett but then went to stay with her sister at Barkingside. She had become friendly with a Sapper Morris from Purfleet Camp and when he left on four days' leave Kate did not return to her sister's home for the four days. This would seem to suggest that she spent the time with him. When she did return home she quarrelled with her sister over her behaviour and left the house again. The following week her body was found on the railway line near Purfleet Camp.

The actual level of sexual contact between soldiers and young unmarried women is impossible to judge, but the issue had been raised earlier in the war when just as the press demonised enemy aliens they also caused a panic over the supposed increasing number of illegitimate births, which led to research into the problem. There had in fact been an organisation founded in relation to this problem called the War Babies and Mothers' League.

There was a report in *The Times* stating that the total of registered illegitimate births each year numbered around 37,000 and no doubt there were many that were not registered. A report in the *Guardian* stated that the number of unmarried mothers in London reported to the War Babies League was 39,000. It was believed that the number of unmarried mothers was perhaps around 30 per cent of the total number of mothers. Mr Ronald O'Neill MP stated in the press that in one borough with a large numbers of soldiers there were 2,000 unmarried pregnant women. The borough was not named so the truth of his

This light-hearted card may have given some people the wrong idea about how cushy life in the forces was.

A very interesting card. It was sent by a soldier named Norman to his family showing where he was billeted. He was in the house with the children outside.

story, as with many of the press stories, could not be checked. The Bishop of Chelmsford had spoken about the large number of troops in his area and he said that there had been a certain amount of evil, meaning sex outside of marriage, but that what had been stated in the press was grossly exaggerated.

The bishop went on to say that they must not allow any sickly sentiment to lead to a relaxation of moral laws. The action of going to the front did not forgive men for sinning at home. Despite his views, the bishop had played a part in gaining a separation allowance for unmarried mothers when the father was serving in the forces.

Rationing was extended and not only food was involved, coal was added to the list. The food shortage led to severe problems in some areas and in Colchester the special constables were needed to control crowds that gathered outside food shops, as on occasions, it looked as though the crowds were about to break into the shops and help themselves.

Another card referring to rationing.

Special constables were also called out in Brentwood when the amount of margarine in the town did not meet the needs of the population. There were what was described as noisy complaints.

George V appealed for economy in the use of food consumption. This appeal was taken up as a movement and cards decorated with purple ribbons were displayed in the windows of some homes stating that the residents were honour bound to observe the king's pledge.

There was an appeal launched when every child in Britain was asked to collect eggs for the wounded soldiers in France. Eggs had reached unprecedented prices at the time and schools were asked to run prize giving for the most successful egg collectors.

Another scheme to help with the food supply was started in Ilford. Waste food was collected from homes for use as pigswill. The idea was begun by Mr R. Middlemas the chairman of Ilford National Service part-time committee. The

A light-hearted rationing postcard with a more serious message.

collections were carried out by church cadets. There were plans to extend the scheme to other areas, as it seemed a very simple but worthwhile occupation.

The big push expected by the Germans was mentioned in the *Essex County Standard* as early as February. There were comments on how preparations were being made by the Germans due to the release of a number of soldiers from the Eastern Front. This was unusual in that when the big push did begin it was at first barely mentioned in the national press. There were other cases of the local press being more daring, for example publishing letters from the front that the nationals would not print due to the horrors they often told of.

When news of the German successes did begin to filter through there was widespread panic in the country. There were fears that the war could in fact be lost and that there could even be a German invasion. It was to be some months before the danger passed and fortunes turned.

There was a great disaster in Shoeburyness in March when a fire broke out at the ranges. There were tons of shells stored there and Shoebury was evacuated as a precaution. Many of the town's inhabitants went to Southend and were put up at the Kursaal. The fire led to the destruction of an enormous amount of shells which were needed in France, especially with the recent German advances.

The success of Essex heroes was celebrated in the *Essex County Standard* with the story of Herbert George Columbine VC who came from Walton on the Naze. It told the story of how he had fatally held off a German attack alone allowing

A class from Bradwell School. Illnesses such as measles often struck and resulted in schools being closed.

BARKING TOWN URBAN DISTRICT COUNCIL ALLOTMENTS COMMITTEE.

A LECTURE

ON THE

Cultivation of Potatoes

AND

Potato Spraying

Will be given at the

Public Baths, East Street,

BARKING,

ON

Friday, Jan. 11, 1918

At 8 p.m.

Lecturer : A. CECIL BARTLETT, Esq.,

Of the Board of Agriculture and Fisheries.

The Lecture will be Illustrated by Lantern Slides.

All Allotment Holders & Potato Growers Invited.

ADMISSION FREE.

Growing food was important enough to warrant lectures on the subject in Barking. The lecture was to be illustrated with lantern slides.

his friends to escape. He was twenty-five years old and left behind his mother, a widow, at a cottage in Crescent Road.

The government setting prices for foodstuffs was in operation by this time and milk was 1s a gallon in May and June, 1s 2d in July and 1s 3d in August and September. Farmers were still far from happy with the price despite its going up.

It seems that despite the government setting price limits and rationing food, there were areas where it was possible to by pass the restrictions. An Inspector Dixon told West Ham magistrates that their area was one of these places. He said that in West Ham it was possible to get meat without coupons if you had the money.

People were coming from other areas to buy meat, as they knew that it was available at a price. Rationing was supposed to give everyone a fair share of what was available, but selling food in this way meant that there was often none left for those entitled to it.

Sugar Distribution to our Regular Customers

Your application form for a Sugar Card must be lodged with your Local Food Committee before October 6th.

If you have not yet lodged your form you should do so immediately.

If you have not received your form for application you can get a copy by asking for one at your local Post Office.

Pure Coffee - - - 1/6
An Ideal Breakfast Beverage.

Pure Coffee - - - - 1/8
Delicious and Refreshing.

INTERNATIONAL STORES
THE BIGGEST GROCERS IN THE WORLD
TEA :: COFFEE :: GROCERIES :: PROVISIONS
I.S. 99.

Despite the main emphasis of this advertisement being sugar rationing, the shop still managed to get some advertising for their coffee in as well.

West Gate Entrance to Barracks, Shoeburyness. 1.

The entrance to Shoeburyness Barracks. The sports field became a tented camp during the war.

The use of aircraft in the war had obviously aroused a great deal of interest among the public. Despite the fact that there was an airfield during the war in Broomfield, when an aircraft was displayed outside the Shire Hall in Chelmsford it attracted large crowds of sightseers. The plane marked the town's Aeroplane Week when it was hoped to raise £50,000 to buy twenty aeroplanes. A special bank was opened at the Shire Hall and the aircraft outside was named Happy Days and had been flown by Major Bishop VC.

Medical treatment was making progress during the war and when Miss Morgan, the matron of the Middlesex Red Cross Hospital at Clacton, welcomed thirty-four members of St Oysth's Red Cross depot to the hospital on a visit, she was proud to show them the new X-ray equipment. The group also spent time speaking to patients and handing out cigarettes. The idea of giving cigarettes to hospital patients shows how ideas have changed.

Advertisements in the local press had no feelings of guilt about using the patriotic feelings of the public to sell their wares. F. Medcalf of Crouch Street, Colchester, informed everyone that cycling was not only the most economical form of travel but in wartime it was also the most patriotic. Hardly surprising then that Medcalf's sold cycles.

There were also numerous advertisements for miracle cures for all sorts of illnesses. A cream called Zam Buk was claimed to cure cuts, bruises, burns, sprains, poisoned wounds, ulcers, pimples, piles, itchy spots and rashes; the list went on and on. Perhaps the most useful claims for the period were the promises that it cured trench sores and barbed wire scratches.

Food was not the only item that was in short supply. The parish council meeting in West Thurrock said that there was a serious lack of coal in the parish and that they needed twenty-five tons a week. They decided to ask the coal controller to get more. They also agreed to relax allotment rules so that allotment holders could keep a pig there.

August saw the first prosecution under the Cultivation of Land Act. William Benjamin Clark, a farmer of Layer, appeared at Colchester Court charged with failing to cultivate part of his land under the order of the Essex War Agricultural Committee. He argued that this was due to a lack of labour but admitted to having seven horses, three men and three boys on his farm. He was fined £25.

Growing food was beginning to be a problem for other reasons as an advertisement in the *Essex County Standard* showed. A hardware shop was advertising the last few available shovels and garden forks for sale. There was also an advertisement for other useful tools. The Dayfield body shield was the ideal protection for men at the front. It weighed only 53¼lb and cost 52s 6d. The advertisement included several letters from pleased customers. There were markedly no complaints from customers that had not found the shield successful.

Sir A.C. Geddes, the Minister of National Service, had appealed to parents and head teachers for the help of boys during the harvest. The calling up of agricultural labourers would leave the rest of industry short of workers. The success of the harvest then relied on boys who were still at school. The ministry had received requests for 17,000 boys and so he appealed to schools to release boys in term time to help out.

Tendring Rural District Food Control Committee asked local children to collect blackberries during their holidays. The payment for this was 2d per pound and the fruit collected was to be sent to the jam factory at Manningtree.

Although the war was still going on there was still a chance for soldiers to enjoy themselves if they were at home by spending a day at the seaside. Unfortunately for one soldier a pleasant day out had the same results as serving in the frontline had for others. Lance Corporal Arthur Lees fell out of a car on the scenic railway at the Kursaal at Southend, suffered a fractured skull, and later died.

There was an accident in Romford that involved an ex-soldier but he was not the victim. The progress made in recognising mental problems in some soldiers by this stage of the war was evident in that Herbert Wall of High Street, Hornchurch, was working for a local timber merchant. Wall had left the Army after suffering from shellshock. Earlier in the war men suffering from the same illness had been shot as cowards. Mr Wall was driving a timber wagon with a large tree on it past Romford Workhouse in Oldchurch Road. He was being assisted by a boy of sixteen, Harry Hazel of Sutton Cottages, Hornchurch. Hazel was walking at the rear of the wagon when a chain came loose trapping him against the wheel and forcing his legs to become tangled in the spokes. He was carried into the workhouse but died soon after.

The Kursaal was a pleasure seekers' playground but was also the site of a tragedy when a soldier died there after falling off a ride.

There was a recruiting rally in Brentwood but not for soldiers, it was to recruit women for the Land Army. It was organised by Mrs Crawshaw and Lady Petrie. There was a guard of honour on the station platform of Girl Guides. Outside the station there was a guard of honour of Boy Scouts. A procession of farm vehicles and carts, decorated and carrying banners encouraging recruitment were ready to travel through the town.

A cortège of the Women's Land Army, Boy Scouts, Girl Guides, children from the Poplar Training School and the band of the Essex Regiment led the vehicles along King's Road and through the High Street attracting the attention of locals as they passed.

The Land Army was not the only service short of recruits. The Essex County Nursing Association meeting stated that they urgently needed more nurses, especially in rural Essex. The shortage was caused by large numbers of women going into national service and the poor wages paid to nurses. More money was being offered to nurses once they were trained and it was hoped that this would turn the profession into a well-paid career and a way of serving the country.

A plea to raise money to buy an aircraft called Brentwood after the town.

BRENTWOOD
Aeroplane Week
begins next
MONDAY

IF, during the week beginning next Monday, the subscriptions from Brentwood for National War Bonds and War Savings Certificates reach the total of £35,000, the authorities will give to an Aeroplane the name of our town.

Think of our civic pride if we read in an official despatch that

the Aeroplane
"BRENTWOOD"

has carried the war into German territory and harried the lines of communication of the foe—perhaps that it has saved Brentwood men from the deadly attack of the Hun, enabling them to return unharmed to their wives and children.

Do your duty during
Brentwood Aeroplane Week

Have your money ready for Monday—ready to buy National War Bonds and War Savings Certificates — ready to help in making Brentwood Aeroplane Week a triumphant, a record success.

Get your Pass Book. See how much money you have in the Bank. Draw the cheque and have it ready to give Brentwood's effort a flying start on Monday morning.

The end of the war did not stop deaths in the forces. Lieutenant Burns of the Royal Air Force died in December 1918. There are several air force personnel buried at Hornchurch who died after the war ended.

There was an aeroplane week in Brentwood in July and if the fundraisers achieved an amount of £35,000, an aeroplane would be named after the town. The total aimed for was less than that hoped to be raised at Chelmsford during their aeroplane week but considering the difference in size of the two towns, Brentwood's aim seemed much more hopeful.

The shortage of food had a great effect on the prices of farms and farming equipment. There was a sale of a farm in Cranham Place, Upminster, after the death of the owner, market gardener Alfred Knight. The sale included a growing crop of potatoes that sold for £46 per acre. Cows also sold for £46 per head. Tumbrel carts went for £28 and a Renault milk van for £145. A Foden steam wagon sold for £1,750.

In September, Frank Fowler, a butcher of Bishop's Stortford, was summonsed by Dunmow Rural Food Committee for offences under the rationing act. Fowler was charged with selling more meat to his customers than their ration coupons allowed. Fowler argued that he had to sell the meat he had before it went bad. He was told that he should have reported any excess to the Food Office who would have told him what to do with it and was found guilty and fined £10.

The exploitation of young women by some soldiers was a common event but one case went much further than just the soldier taking advantage of the woman. Arthur Mulford, aged thirty-one, a gunner in the Royal Canadian Horse Artillery,

Upminster was still very rural during the war but the chapel building on the left is still there.

ended up in court charged with signing a false notice of marriage at Romford Register Office. Mulford had asked Constance Gold of Romford to marry him in January 1917. She had a child by him in August that year. It seems that he had no intention of marrying her as he was already married. However, a witness had accompanied him to the registrar's office and he had no choice but to sign the document. He was later arrested in Kent. His wife's sister was in court as a witness against him.

There was another example of how the war was affecting some people who were not fighting in it. Mrs Lizzie Wright of Romford was charged with strangling one of her grandchildren, a young baby. It was stated that she had been acting strangely and was worried about her sons who were fighting at the front.

Although the end of the war may have been in sight, there was still a need to carry on to the end and in fact past the end as things were not going to get back to normal straight away once the fighting stopped. It did not help then when the railway workers went on strike in September. The strike began in Wales but affected London and Essex when train drivers and firemen from Stratford joined the strikes.

Hospitals had been opened everywhere during the war and the Upminster Auxiliary Military Hospital was reported to be doing excellent work. There was an appeal in the *Essex Times* for locals to supply enough beetroot, carrots, parsnips and onions to last them through the winter.

By this time the Spanish Flu epidemic had begun to hit home and there were numerous reports of deaths in the local press. Elizabeth Young, aged twenty-three of Barnyard Cottages, Ardleigh Green, had been suffering from the illness for three days before her condition worsened and she died.

The Royal Forest Hotel, Chingford, was wanted as a home for ex-soldiers but there were problems raising enough money to buy it.

A letter from Dr Thresh, the county medical officer for health from Chelmsford was published in the *Essex Times*. He said that he had been asked many times everyday about what could be done to help stop the spread of the influenza illness. He answered that the local government board pamphlet on the subject was helpful but had missed out one important aspect: the spraying of areas where people who might have the illness had been with disinfectant. This was especially important in places such as schools and places of entertainment. Dr Thresh then went on to list a number of suitable disinfectants that were available for this purpose.

Despite widespread illness and lack of food the end of the war was greeted with joy by everyone. At the news of the armistice, crowds thronged the streets of

A menu for a celebration dinner for the Sportsman's Battalion and their return to Blighty.

Colchester waving Union Jacks. The news was posted in the windows of local newspaper offices. The Colchester Town Council was meeting at the time and the mayor dressed in his robes to come out onto the town hall balcony.

For some the war had been over for some time. The past year had been a difficult time for the men returning wounded from the trenches. Any form of treat that could be given to them was gratefully received. A steam launch, *His Majesty*, had been used by the Red Cross to take wounded men on trips along the Thames. They had carried out seventy-eight trips in the past year taking 7,111 wounded men on these excursions, along with 100 nurses. Another steam launch, the *Gaiety*, had been run by a fund raised locally and had taken 8,556 wounded men and 122 nurses on similar trips.

Many wounded men were still being treated in workhouses. Romford Union in November had 290 inmates with 102 boarded out. There were also seventy-eight wounded men in the military block.

The end of the war did not stop rationing nor the attempts to evade it and the price limits set by the government. There was a long list of reported abuses of the rules in late November.

Charles Baines of Belgrave Market, Ilford, was charged with selling coffee for more than 1s 6d a pound. He was fined 25s. Arthur Horner of Ley Street, Ilford, was charged with selling condensed milk at an excessive price. He charged 1s 3d for a tin of Nestlé's condensed milk. He was fined 20s. George Smith of Aldborough Road, Seven Kings, was charged with selling tinned meat without taking the necessary coupons from the customer. He was also fined 20s.

The flu epidemic was hitting all local areas and in West Ham the medical officer of health reported on the five weeks ending on 2 November as having 748 deaths in the borough and 91 outside. Of these, 379 were male and 469 female and 67 of these were under the age of one. That gave a child death rate of 32 per cent per thousand whereas in the previous year it had been 12.3 per cent. The death figures for the past seven weeks and their equivalent rates from the previous year were also given:

	1917	1918
5 October	49	46
12 October	55	71
19 October	55	113
26 October	60	201
2 November	65	379
9 November	44	376
16 November	52	285

In December new rules were passed to try to limit the spread of the disease. Places of entertainment were limited to a maximum of three hours per show. There then had to be at least a half an hour's interval before the next show. During the interval the venue had to be well ventilated.

As part of the peace celebrations the fleet visited Southend in July 1919.

A souvenir card of the fleet's visit to Southend.

Policy $\frac{F}{1}$ Nº 048482

Office of Issue :—

Number 30404   Rank

Name

(In full, Christian names first. In the case of women state
whether Mrs. or Miss)

Miss

Unit and Regiment

Date of Birth 20/3/1898

Industrial Group

Trade Housemaid

Classification No.

OUT-OF-WORK DONATION POLICY
(H.M. Forces).

This Policy is of no value except to the person to whom it is issued.
For Instructions and Conditions as to receipt of Out-of-Work Donation
see pages 2 and 4 of cover.

F D. 9

(33955) Wt. 19601/1334 20,000 9-19 W B & L

An out-of-work donation policy; they obviously knew what was coming once men left the forces.

Holder's Signature

The first date on which this Policy will be available is..**21 NOV 1919**
(this is the date on which the holder may begin to sign the coupons herein).

This Policy is available for twelve months from the end of furlough. Therefore, it
will not be available after..................................**23 NOV 1920**

The number of weeks of donation which may be drawn up to and including the last
above-mentioned date is twenty-six weeks at the rate of 29s. a week for men and 25s. a
week for women, subject to the conditions printed on this Policy. A supplementary
donation is payable in respect of dependent children under 15 years of age at the
following rates per week :—

6s. for first child and 3s. in respect of each additional child.

HOW TO OBTAIN OUT-OF-WORK DONATION.

1. On becoming unemployed and desiring to obtain donation you must lodge this
Policy at an Employment Exchange or at a Branch Employment Office of the Ministry of
Labour. (The address of the nearest Exchange or Branch Office can be obtained at any
Post Office.)

2. On attending at an Exchange or Branch Office to claim donation you must also
take with you your discharge papers and there sign the form of claim to donation in this
Policy.

3. So long as you are unemployed and desirous of drawing donation you must attend
daily, or in certain exceptional cases less frequently, between certain hours which will be
notified to you at an Exchange or Branch Office for the purpose of signing in this Policy a
declaration of unemployment.

4. Until you desire to claim out-of-work donation you must retain this Policy in
your own possession.

The pages show how much information had to be given to get the benefits that had been paid for.

The end of the war led to widespread unemployment even among the able-bodied soldiers returning from the war. As well as the large numbers of men returning from the Army, work in areas such as munitions obviously tailed off almost immediately. Those who were disabled had even less chance of finding work of any kind.

Organisations to help ex-soldiers began to try to help. The Comrades of War was a non-political organisation formed in 1917 to help those who had left the

Can you give this Ex-Serviceman a job? or help him by buying this bill.

Disabled Soldier's Appeal

I did hear my country calling
    In her darkest hour of strife
And was ready then to help her,
    Ready—aye— to give my life.

Caring not for home or pleasure,
    Parent, wife nor children small,
Thinking how I best could serve her,
    Answering to my country's call.

I have served my country faithfully,
    And have given of my best,
In this war for Right and Freedom,
    Facing death—and worse with jest.

I have seen my comrades falling,
    'Midst the storm of shot and shell,
And have laughed and sung whilst standing
    At the very gates of hell.

On the cliffs of Gallipoli,
    Or the stricken fields of France,
'Neath the scorching sun of Asia,
    Taking every risk and chance.

Risking life and limbs whilst " Slackers "
    'Neath their precious War Badge hide,
Why should they not take their chances
    In the roll of battles tide ?

Yet in spite of sacrifices,
    I am told that once again,
Both my King and country need me—
    I shall not let them call in vain.

The distress of some old soldiers after the war was shown by this printed poem that disabled ex-soldiers often tried to sell in pubs. It was no more than a form of begging that they had been reduced to.

SURRENDER OF GERMAN FLEET
GERMAN U. BOATS AT HARWICH

German U-boats sailed into Harwich Harbour to surrender after the war.

Army. Along with three other organisations they were predecessors of the British Legion, which was formed in 1921. The comrades did their best to obtain pensions for those who were injured and also trained some ex-soldiers in different trades.

SIX

AFTER THE WAR

It was to be well into 1919 before many of the men finally came home from the forces. The slow pace of repatriation was partly caused by the need of an army of occupation in Germany. It did cause problems as the men just wanted to get home. This led to some disruption and in one camp in Canada, Kimmel Military Camp, there was a riot and some deaths due to the men being forced to remain in the Army. Many of the old camps were again full of soldiers. One Essex camp was used as a demobilisation centre. Purfleet Barracks found itself full of soldiers who were being sent home.

Celebration of the heroes' return often took the form of a dinner held by the local council. These dinners were usually held in local schools and in Weeley they had the novel idea of printing the roll of honour of those who died in the menu. Whether this put the men who did come back off their meals wasn't mentioned. In November, Dunmow Council held a dinner for the 230 men who came back. 84 did not return.

The local authority did not always pay for the celebrations. At Little Clacton there was a collection to pay for the Peace Celebrations. £59 16s 9d was raised, most of which was spent on the celebrations. The money left, £8 10s, was donated to St Dustan's Clinic for blind servicemen.

There were calls to look after the men who had been fighting and had survived. Rear-Admiral Lionel Halsey made a speech saying that it was the obligation of every person to ensure that the men who had been fighting were properly cared for and their future assured. There was a plan to acquire the Epping Forest Hotel in Chingford as a convalescent home for ex-servicemen. This would cost £10,000 but so far they had only collected £500.

The belief that England would be a better place to live after the men of the country had fought a war to save the land turned out to be far from the truth. The vicar of Hornchurch, the Revd Charles Steer, gave an example of how there seemed to be little effort on the behalf of Romford Council to do anything for the people, including the families of and in some cases the men themselves who had fought in the war. Steer described how he had seen two families evicted from cottages that they had lived in for twenty and seventeen years respectively.

War memorials were raised in numerous places. This one is still in place in Shenfield railway station.

A memorial to Kenneth Chetwynd Harvey-George in Barking Church. Sergeant Harvey-George was wounded and gassed twice in 1915 and in May 1917. He died the following month.

The reason for this was that the farmer wanted them for two of his men. Both families had nowhere else to go. Steer made a suggestion to the council that old Army huts could be used to house these and other families and so reduce homelessness and overcrowding.

The council, after much correspondence with numerous groups, decided to move some huts from Army camps to other sites for families. The War Office stopped them being used as it seems they would rather they stood empty. Then it seems that the council had to make sure that the huts that were still standing on Grey Towers Camp were not occupied by squatters as other camps had been in other parts of the country.

Meanwhile the sub-committee of housing of the Essex County Council reported that 2,170 new cottages were needed in the county at once and that 1,982 existing cottages would have to be condemned. This showed the poor conditions that many families were living in.

Memorial plaque in Barking Church.

The committee went on to state that if any substantial amount of the needed cottages were to be erected within the next two years, it was essential that some central controlling body should supervise and co-ordinate the work.

The lack of housing for the poor was not a problem that the better off suffered from. Many of the large estates in the county were now being used to build houses on as a way of making money. Some of the old Army camps were included in this.

In Gidea Park, the Romford Garden Suburb had been started before the war, covering the grounds of the old Gidea Hall, which was opposite Hare Hall Camp and was owned by Herbert Raphael MP. He had been based at the camp as a member of the Sportsman's Battalion. A competition had been held among architects to find the best man who could design houses that would cost £350 or £500. The prize was 1,000 guineas. There were around 14,000 families that moved out to what was described as 'Further London' in the *Graphic* newspaper and it was also said that it was only by raising the architectural level of dwellings that substantial improvement in the outer Metropolis could be hoped for.

After the war, the grounds of the Hare Hall Camp were also used to build on, but again the houses were mainly similar to those on the Gidea Hall site. The houses built were not within the price range of most of the men returning from the war.

Grey Towers in Hornchurch was to suffer from a similar fate, although in this case the land was sold off in small parcels and builders built smaller, more modest houses for sale. This process was repeated on many estates throughout the county but often the houses built were for sale and were beyond the means of most of the men returning from the war who needed houses to rent, not to buy.

There was an interesting item in the *Manchester Guardian* relating to the building of houses concerning the difficulty of building from brick in Manchester. The local public health committee were considering building concrete houses but could only find examples of these in Braintree.

They reported that the houses were built entirely of concrete blocks; even the floors were concrete and the roofs, which were flat. They were all made on the site and had three bedrooms with a parlour kitchen and even a bathroom. The only timber in the house was the doors.

They were built for a public utility company by the Unit Concrete Company and were 25 per cent cheaper than brick-built houses. They seem to have been quite modern for the time and sound similar to the houses built later by the Bata Shoe Company for their employees at East Tilbury.

The materials used for new housing was a worry for many people. When new houses were built in small villages there were concerns that using the cheapest materials would cause the new houses to stand out and look out of place.

There were plans to build smaller more affordable houses for rent but these were to be built by local authorities and they did not move as quickly as private builders. The government eventually realised that the thousands of houses that were needed were not going to return economical rents until some years after the

The memorial plaque to the Sportsman's Battalion in the church at Hornchurch.

war and suggested that they be responsible for 75 per cent of the shortfall in the rents while the local authorities take responsibility for the other 25 per cent.

There had been a bill passed by parliament just before the end of the war giving local government boards the power to build houses for the working classes during the war and up to twelve months afterwards. This was in situations where the county had not taken the steps to do so. The bill also allowed up to eighty years to pay back the money borrowed to build the houses.

An article in *The Times* in February 1919 explained the problems that stopped the building of houses for the working classes. It reported that along the north bank of the Thames there were 167,911 people living in overcrowded conditions, in Poplar, Stepney and West Ham. The whole of London gained advantage from the works of the docks stretching from the Tower down to Tilbury but each area could not afford to pay to build their own houses. They called for an adequate housing scheme in rural South Essex to solve this overcrowding.

It was impossible for the affected boroughs to deal with this problem by building all the houses needed themselves, but they called for all the other boroughs who benefited from the docks to help pay for them. The result of this was the building of the Becontree Estate in what was then the open spaces of Dagenham, paid for by the London County Council in the early 1920s.

As well as a lack of places to live, the men coming home found that they also had few jobs between them. Even able-bodied men were finding it hard to get

Although only a small village at the time of the war, Aveley's memorial is very grand and very well kept and is surrounded by ornamental railings.

jobs. Those disabled by the war found it almost impossible. As well as the lack of jobs there were also a number of problems in that many of the unions were pressing for decent working conditions and rates of pay for their members.

A meeting of the Farm Workers' Union decided to ask for a wage of 50s for a forty-four hour week. Politicians described many of the men involved in these demands as Bolsheviks. It seems that the men who had saved the country had in many cases become a liability now that they wanted a decent living after living through the horrors of the trenches.

The Revd F. Adams of Doddinghurst Rectory, Brentwood, wrote to *The Times* and described how a parishioner asked him to sign an application for the out of work gratuity. When he asked why the man was out of work he answered that farmers would not employ him, as he was a member of the union. Also the

Some places decided on different styles of memorials such as this one in the porch of the church in Buckhurst Hill.

gratuity for him and his children was much more than he would be paid for working. He was obviously then not going to try very hard to find work.

This would seem to have been an isolated case as there was a large-scale protest against the Leyton and Leytonstone War Pension Committee who were accused of making it impossible to obtain a decent pension from them. The protestors quoted one case of a blind man who was getting 10s a week when the recommended level for a blind man was 20s. The committee argued that the levels set were recommendations and they were not forced to abide by them. They always seemed, however, to use the discretion allowed them in their favour by granting a lower amount.

Some men found ways around the low wages that were on offer for those who could get a job. Arthur Antill, aged twenty-nine, of Edward Road, Walthamstow, was charged with obtaining three sums of money from the Ministry of Labour fraudulently. He had deposited an insurance policy with the labour exchange and got three payments totalling £5 1s 4d. He was in fact working at Lacey and Company automobile engineers at the time. He was earning £2 2s a week and paid 8s travel and could not manage on the money he was paid. He was sent to prison for six weeks' hard labour.

It was not only men who found work hard to come by or difficult to stay at. A young woman wrote to the *Essex Times* to describe her work as a nurse at Romford Infirmary. The hours were from 7.00 a.m. to 6.30 p.m. with an hour for lunch. Lunch had to be provided by the nurse. For this they were paid 35s a week. They had no rest, apart from the lunch break, and every thing was controlled by ridiculous amounts of red tape.

The memorial at Clacton.

There were training courses run in some areas for men coming home from the war. However as the men completed the courses and still could not find jobs, the courses began to disappear.

There were still food shortages and in Barking the Food Control Committee stated that in one month 1,285 people had changed their choice of retailer. They had also issued 575 new ration books to returning soldiers. They also called for stocks of food to be put aside for children in the case of an emergency due to the widespread labour unrest.

It was not only food that was still in short supply. A mother explained the reason that she could not send her son to school: the boy had already been suffering from bronchitis and had got his boots wet. As there was no coal she could not dry his boots and so kept him at home.

The end of the war had not led to an end of the military in the county. There were some strange events related to these soldiers. One of the men from the New Zealand camp at Grey Towers was attacked for no reason outside the Golden Lion public house in Romford. The attack was witnessed by a policeman who agreed that the attack had been unprovoked. The commanding officer of the camp stated in court that there had been a growing number of attacks on his men while they were out in the local areas.

The evacuation of the trenches did not stop deaths from occurring among servicemen. Lt Arthur Simmons was flying a Sopwith Camel from Hainault Airfield to Hornchurch when he lost control of the plane, which crashed, causing his death. The cemetery at Hornchurch contains the graves of a number of airmen who died shortly after the war ended.

Whatever the difficulties of those who did come back, there were a number who did not. The whereabouts of many of these men was unknown. An advertisement in the *Essex Times* showed this clearly. Mr E.C. Grange of Plaistow had placed an appeal for knowledge of the whereabouts of his son, Rifleman E.W. Grange of the 8th Platoon 8th London Regiment. He had gone into action on September the 8th or 9th at Epehy and had been posted as missing the same day.

Then there were calls to commemorate those who did not come back. Although there were some war memorials before this time they were very few and far between. They were normally found in garrison towns or in large cities and were mainly from the Boer War period.

WAR MEMORIAL AND CASTLE, COLCHESTER.

The memorial at Colchester cost more than £3,000 but was still much less than the total amount raised to pay for it.

In the immediate post-war period war memorials appeared in most towns and villages. They now seem commonplace but were, before this period, mainly unknown. These memorials also appeared in places of worship and public and private establishments. Public schools had their old boys' memorials but they also appeared in railway stations, breweries and factories. These did not always take the form of a memorial stone. Some churches had warriors' chapels, a cross or a simple inscribed tablet. Wickford commemorated its twenty-nine dead in the Memorial Nurses' Home in Southend Road. Harold Wood had a Memorial Hall. The Colchester Royal Grammar School had a Memorial Swimming Baths.

One of the greener ideas that seems to have been before its time was at Downham near Billericay. Sixteen oak trees were planted, one for each of the sixteen villagers killed in the war. They were planted by the closest living relative of each of the deceased. Each tree had a commemorative tablet with details of the man and his place of death attached with telephone wire brought from France.

Not everyone agreed with the erection of monuments for the dead. In May 1918 at a meeting of the London Labour Party, Fred Bramley said that it was not expensive monuments that were needed for the dead, but to pull down the slums and build decent houses for their wives and children.

There was some concern aired over the erection of war memorials inside churches. One of the people to voice these views was the Bishop of Chelmsford. In an article in *The Times* it was reported that he wrote to Essex churchwardens reminding them to apply for a faculty before placing memorials in the church. The bishop had seen several examples where memorials had been placed with no regard to architecture or the items that were removed to make way for them. Churchwardens were only trustees of the buildings and had no right to change things at their discretion.

The memorials have interesting variations that show the views of those who were responsible for organising the monuments. Some have a simple alphabetical list of those who died. In more class-conscious areas officers are listed first, in order of superiority and include the rank of the deceased. This firmly fixed the person's position in society for all time. Some even have an order of regiment with the more elite ones such as the guards coming before the service battalions formed just for the war.

There was nationwide interest in the new memorials especially from sculptors who suddenly found their services in demand. The sculptor Mr W. Reynolds Stephens wrote in a letter to *The Times* in April saying that if the nation wishes to do the greatest honour to its dead heroes then memorials must have a vivid mental appeal and be made from the most imperishable materials available.

The larger towns could of course erect the grander memorials, usually paid for by public subscription. In Colchester the plan was to raise £3,000 for a memorial, a huge amount in those days. In fact they raised £7,599. There was a plan to spend the excess of the collection on building a memorial wing at the hospital but increased building costs made this impossible.

The South Ockendon memorial is quite modest, as one would expect in what at the time was a small village.

The Royal Academy invited sculptors to send in models of their ideas for memorials. They then held an exhibition of the ideas at the Victoria & Albert Museum. The Colchester committee responsible for the memorial chose one by Mr H.C. Fehr, a local man who had been born in Forest Gate. Mr Fehr also designed several other war memorials around the country.

In line with Mr Reynolds' views on imperishable materials, the Colchester memorial was constructed from Portland stone, granite and bronze for the statues. It was erected in June 1922. The council also published a souvenir book of the First World War.

Whether the money spent on such memorials could have been put to a better purpose for the living is debatable. What they have achieved is to remind people of the men who made the ultimate sacrifice for their country. They also introduced a method whereby those who died in later conflicts could also be added to them. Wherever you are, you are never far from a monument that reminds you of what you owe those brave men from the past.

BIBLIOGRAPHY

Banks, T. & Chell, R., *With The 10th Essex In France*, Burt, 1921

Benham, *Benham's Colchester: A History and Guide*, Benham & Co. Ltd, 1946

Burgoyne, J., *Weeley and Weeley Heath*, Millstone, 1999

Dowsett, D., *Dunmow through The Ages*, Dowsett, 1970

Everitt, B., *The Story of Moore Brothers*, Everitt, 1998

Foley, M., *Front-Line Thames*, The History Press, 2008

Gerrard, A., *Butterflies & Coalsmoke*, Susan Abrahams, 1988

Hall, P., *Wickford*, Chalford, 1996

Harper, A., *Burnham-on-Crouch AD 2000*, Burnham-on-Crouch Council, 2000

Harper, G., *Warley Magna to Great Warley*, Dickens, 1984

Hunt, E. (ed), *Colchester War Memorial Souvenir*, Essex Telegraph Ltd, 1923

Lucas, P., *Basildon*, Phillimore, 1991

Mannox, B., *Hornchurch and the New Zealand Connection*, London Borough of Havering,
    1993

Marlow, J. (ed), *Women and the Great War*, Virago, 1998

Martin, G., *The Story Of Colchester*, Benham, 1959

Maxwell, D., *Unknown Essex*, Bodley Head, 1925

Mays, S., *Reuben's Corner*, Robin Clark, 1981

Orford, M., *The Shoebury Story*, Ian Henry, 2000

Perfect, C., *Hornchurch During The Great War*, Benham & Co. Ltd, 1920

Phillips, A., *Colchester: A History*, Phillimore, 2004

Reynolds, R., *Thurrock – The Great War*, Brent, 1998

Rhodes, L. & Abnett K., *Foul Deeds and Suspicious Deaths In Barking, Dagenham &
    Chadwell Heath*, Wharncliffe Books, 2007

Scott, W., *Coryton,* Mobil, 1982

Searle, M., *Down The Line To Southend*, Baton, 1984

Smith, V., *Coalhouse Fort*, Essex County Council, 1985

Tames, R., *Barking Past,* Historical Publications, 2002

Thomas, H., *Under Storm's Wing*, Carcanet, 1988

Thomas, O., *Childhood Memories of Hornchurch*, London Borough of Havering, 1991

Thorogood, J. (ed), *The Last All Clear*, Sarsen, 1989

Torry, G., *Chelmsford Through The Ages*, East Anglian Magazine, 1977

Walker, K., *Clacton-on-Sea in Old Photographs*, Sutton, 1995

Weaver, L., *The Harwich Story*, Weaver, 1975

Yearsley, I., *Essex Events*, Phillimore, 1999

——, *A History Of Southend*, Phillimore, 2001

Articles, Documents and Newspapers

Barking, East Ham & Ilford Advertiser, 8 August 1914, 19 September 1914, 6 March 1915, 7 August 1915, 1 January 1916, 22 April 1916, 7 April 1917, 14 April 1917, 18 August 1917, 13 October 1917, 20 July 1918, 28 September 1918

Christy, M., *Quarterly Journal of the Meteorological Society,* Vol XL, Oct 1916

Essex County Standard, 3 January 1916, 8 February 1916, 9 January 1917, 14 April 1917, 21 February 1918, 16 August 1918

Essex Record Office Document: (D/DS 206/121) Postcard of Cliffs at Leigh, (J/P 12/6) Investigations into those with German associations, (D/P 80/28/2 Little Clacton Parish Activities, (D/DU 672/4) The Diary of Robert Taylor Bull, (T/Z 467/1) Memoirs of Kynochtown-Catherine and Dorothy Mackintosh

Essex Times, 1 January 1916, 22 April 1916, 12 August 1916, 6 January 1917, 24 February 1917, 10 March 1917, 26 May 1917, 7 July 1917, 28 July 1917, 13 October 1917, 3 November 1917, 26 January 1918, 23 March 1918, 18 May 1918, 15 June 1918

Evans B., 'The Soldiers Come to Hare Street', *Romford Record* , no. 39, 2005/06

Graphic, 6 May 1911

Imperial War Museum, Ferrie, Captain W.S. (03/19/1)

Manchester Guardian, 28 December 1914, 17 April 1914, 23 February 1915, 10 May 1915, 13 September 1915, 10 November 1915, 11 January 1916, 27 October 1917, 23 February 1918

Observer, 1 November 1914, 18 April 1915, 27 June 1915, 3 September 1916, 24 September 1916, 19 November 1916

Perfect, C., 'Control and Rationing of Food 1917-1919', *Havering History Review,* no. 17, 2001

The Times, 5 February 1915, 11 May 1915, 13 May 1915, 26 August 1915, 21 April 1917, 1 May 1917, 13 August 1917, 4 April 1919, 2 January 1920

Warren, J., 'Scouts and Two World Wars', *Havering History Review,* no. 17, 2001

INDEX